# Art of
# Letting Go

## Releasing Control and Finding Freedom in Surrender

*(A Guide to Forgive Yourself Build Resilience and Discipline Your Mind to Become the Best You)*

## Richard Lamberton

Published By **Phil Dawson**

# Richard Lamberton

All Rights Reserved

*Art of Letting Go: Releasing Control and Finding Freedom in Surrender (A Guide to Forgive Yourself Build Resilience and Discipline Your Mind to Become the Best You)*

**ISBN   978-1-9994256-4-7**

Legal & Disclaimer

The information contained in this book is not designed to replace or take the place of any form of medicine or professional medical advice. The information in this book has been provided for educational & entertainment purposes only.

The information contained in this book has been compiled from sources deemed reliable, and it is accurate to the best of the Author's knowledge; however, the Author cannot guarantee its accuracy and validity and cannot be held liable for any errors or omissions. Changes are periodically made to this book. You must consult your doctor or get professional medical advice before using any of the suggested remedies, techniques, or information in this book.

Table Of Contents

# Chapter 1: The Stages Of Heartbreak

Understanding the Emotional Rollercoaster

Your coronary heart has been ripped from your chest, torn to pieces, and stomped on through the use of your ex in more than one heavy boots. Okay, maybe now not simply, however that's sincerely the manner it feels inside the raw, earliest days after a devastating breakup.

When your partner first utters the dreadful terms "I anticipate we need to interrupt up," or "I don't love you anymore," you revel in like your international is imploding. Nothing makes revel in. This relationship modified into everything to you actually the day prior to this, and now all at once it's over? Your mind reels, frantic with questions. How want to this take vicinity? What went incorrect? Is there whatever you can have accomplished in a outstanding way to shop topics? You'd good deal your soul to the satan himself if you concept it can undo this split and bring lower decrease back the one you love.

But it cannot be undone. A breakup, with the resource of its very nature, is jarring and disorienting. One day your life is on direction with a need to percent it with, the following day the track has disappeared proper from under your toes, leaving you misplaced and compelled approximately the way to circulate ahead on my own.

It's extra than simply feeling sad or dissatisfied - you are completely devastated for your middle. You revel in empty, aimless. You may replay each second of the relationship time and again on your thoughts, torturing yourself with what-ifs and if-onlys. You preserve desperately to the faint preference that your ex may exchange their mind in case you say the right phrases or do the right detail. Calling them continuously, displaying up unannounced, making dramatic pleas - you're willing to do just about some thing to turn decrease again time.

But part of you is aware of, irrespective of it all that the connection you as soon as had is long gone for suitable. This first degree of heartbreak is all about denial moving to despair. But the avalanche of feelings has high-quality certainly began out.

The Volcanic Eruption

After the initial shock and denial subside, the ache you've tamped down erupts with volcanic pressure. Hot anger replaces cold disbelief.

You rage toward the injustice of all of it - how dare they damage your heart and shatter your desires without a second idea! You need to manual them to damage as badly as you do now, to scream and cry and unleash fury like a wildfire until there can be no longer something left to burn.

Of direction, appearing on the ones impulses usually handiest leaves you feeling greater ashamed and regretful. But the volcanic feelings demand a few type of release in advance than they honestly consume you.

So you sob into your pillow until your eyes burn. You mag and not using a end in sight actually to untangle the infinite knots on your coronary coronary heart. Maybe you be part of up for kickboxing commands, welcoming the hazard to literally kick and punch your emotions out. Stomping your ft, clenching your jaw, balling your fists - your body mirrors the inner tumult, equipped to fight but collapsing inward at the identical time.

This volcanic degree is critical for venting your pent-up feelings so you can in the long run circulate earlier. Embrace it as an important part of the recovery adventure.

The Mourning Fog

After the eruption comes the mourning fog. A heavy disappointment descends like a blanket, muffling the arena round you. Just getting faraway from bed feels now not viable some days.

You mourn what is long long beyond - the intimate talks, the amusing adventures, the goals for the future you shared. You mourn your nice pal, your closest confidante, your steady haven from the storms of the arena.

Profound loneliness devices in. You pass over the quality topics, like having a person to percentage little internal jokes with or cuddle at night time. The space they used to occupy feels so painfully empty now.

The fog slows the entirety down and conceals any enjoy of which means or cause. Each day bleeds mindlessly into the subsequent. Rather than raging tears, you cry quiet, determined tears - no longer for the relationship you could't get again, however to your misplaced self.

This mourning fog is a critical duration of adjustment. By honoring your grief, the fog slowly lifts on its private timetable. You trust that you cannot pressure the mild to move back earlier than you have got completely venerated the loss in its aching entirety.

Emerging From The Fog

One morning, you recognise the fog has thinned ever so slightly. You seize a glimpse of daytime peeking via the clouds. Bursts of laughter from buddies stir a few issue faintly within you. You sip your coffee and phrase it in reality has taste over again.

Clarity starts brightening small wallet of your thoughts and coronary coronary heart. You begin seeing property you have got been unaware of earlier than - how poorly your ex in fact treated you, diffused purple flags you made excuses for or brushed off.

You apprehend that as a lot as this loss hurts, selecting a person who should no longer comprehend your properly actually well worth is the finest self-betrayal of all. This revelation empowers righteous anger to reduce thru the disappointment and self-pity.

Slowly the fog burns off for top. You take deep breaths of crisp air. Colors seem extra colorful, track more transferring. You laugh and genuinely advise it. Curiosity approximately life tickles you yet again.

You however have tough moments, however they bypass faster. You save you clinging to fantasies of reconciliation. The beyond loosens its grip, freeing you up for a hopeful future.

You have crossed via the darkest depths of grief into the moderate of opportunity. Now the adventure shifts from letting go to searching in advance.

Dancing With Discomfort

But remembering the way to stand on your very private  ft after relying on a person else for goodbye can feel uncomfortable and unsteady. Moving on is often  steps in advance, one step again.

Loneliness necessarily no matter the reality that washes over you. Random reminiscences ambush you at the identical time as you least count on it. You query if you'll ever discover love once more.

Instead of resisting the ones hurts when they stand up, you meet them with radical gentleness and popularity. You soothe loneliness via accomplishing out to supportive pals and family. You honor lingering grief while it surfaces, whilst moreover reassuring your coronary coronary coronary heart that new happiness exists.

The sting slowly lessens each time as you construct self guarantee in your emotional resilience. You accept as true with you have got were given the energy to dance gracefully with the ones tough feelings after they return.

Letting go, it appears, isn't always a difficult and rapid vacation spot however an ongoing exercise. Some days go together with the go with the flow without difficulty, even as one among a type days you stumble. But you maintain leaning in the proper course - into self-care, into network, into the existing of every new 2nd.

One foot within the the front of the opportunity, you circulate bravely onward.

## Turning Inward

In the stillness after loss, you've got the space to word what your non-public soul yearns for. Not what your ex desired, no longer what society expects, but what makes your spirit come alive.

You rediscover dormant passions and goals. Long-disregarded interests like portray, hiking, or creating a tune pull at your interest. You join up for night time education and workshops just because they intrigue you.

You think a good buy less about "alleged to" and start asking "why now not?" greater frequently as a substitute. Daring comes less complex because of the reality you have got were given plenty less left to lose now. Each small act of braveness expands your self assure.

By listening inner, your destiny well-known itself. Through turning inward, you boom a compass guiding you to a lifestyles genuinely your non-public.

Glimmers From The Ashes

Walking through the fireside transforms you. You see your inner slight in a cutting-edge way.

Strength you in no manner knew you possessed emerges like steel solid from flames. You apprehend heartbreak's gadgets - empathy, resilience, self-consider. Adversity introduces you to your self.

You apprehend relationships do not whole you - you had been already whole. What a accomplice have to do is growth your mild, no longer be the deliver of it. Healthy love complements existence without eclipsing all else.

From the ashes, glimmers of a appreciably beautiful new lifestyles take shape - one where your voice doesn't pass dim to make others comfortable. You speak your truth with boldness. You apprehend your properly really worth deep down.

You burned away what turn out to be false. Now exceptional what's real stays - a better, more discerning coronary coronary heart; a renewed spirit for adventure; a faith in yourself that withstands all storms.

The Phoenix Takes Flight

One morning you open your eyes and without a doubt enjoy extraordinary. Lighter. Hopeful. Ready for some component.

You personal clarity that this breakup does no longer define you. It's really one bankruptcy in the epic tale despite the fact that being written. This loss prepared you for destinies you could't yet accept as actual with.

So you open your wings. You inhabit the pleasure of in recent times with out borrowing against day after today. You giggle, dance, sing like no person's searching. You stay with wild gratitude, wolf-like devotion, and lion-fierce authenticity.

Whenever darkness creeps lower lower lower back in, you do not resist it or flee from it. You breathe thru it until it passes, every time spiraling upwards all once more.

You have made it through the crucible. Your steps gain self assurance, your wings benefit strength. One day you appearance inside the mirror and glimpse the phoenix developing from the ashes wherein a heartbroken soul as soon as stood.

You had been made anew. Your eyes shine colourful with hope, understanding, and freedom. The destiny stands in advance than you, extra radiant than ever. You are ready to leap.

## Chapter 2: Allow Yourself To Grieve

Don't Bottle Up Your Feelings

Your coronary coronary coronary heart is shattered. You sense including you've been punched inside the gut one hundred instances. Moving on seems truly no longer possible whilst you can slightly breathe through the thick fog of grief.

Every tune reminds you of what you out of vicinity. You harm down crying randomly throughout the day. The nights are even worse, plagued through burdened insomnia or dreams approximately your ex that experience so real you forget about for a 2nd you awoke by myself.

This sorrow seems infinite, so huge that it might surely swallow you complete. But face up to the temptation to suppress it or faux you experience better than you do. Allow your self to grieve honestly, with out judgment or disgrace. This is the way you flow into through grief instead of very last caught in it.

## Honor the Anguish

The give up of a dating merits to be mourned. Love is not disposable or meaningless. If it without a doubt touched your soul, its loss will cut deep. The more the love, the greater excruciating its absence.

Feeling struggling suggests the intensity of your capability for connection. You unapologetically honor this ache, irrespective of how overwhelming. Beating yourself up for not "getting over it" quicker great causes greater needless struggling. Love and grief glide from the same everlasting supply inner you.

Have compassion for all of the waves of turmoil crashing inside. Cry out the ocean of tears begging for launch. Scream right right right into a pillow when the anger surges. Let your feelings glide like a river to cleanse your internal panorama.

This honoring is holy ritual, cute in its rawness. Little by using way of little, the waters cleanse you and repair equilibrium. Be affected person with the machine.

Lean on Your Tribe

You need assist now more than ever. Don't isolate your self in the cave of unhappiness. Reach out to the individuals who sincerely deal with you and allow them to into your global.

Share vulnerably approximately what you're going thru. They obtained't decide you for the flood of feelings or for backsliding on your development. They can in reality hold space on your true enjoy with compassion.

Laughing through tears with near buddies does wonders for lifting the spirits. Therapy provides professional guidance so that you can vent thoroughly in a judgment-loose area. Support groups join you with others strolling this path too.

You draw energy from your network, which empowers you to maintain moving ahead. You apprehend you are in no manner by myself, now not even on your darkest moments.

## Let It Out Creatively

Writing, track, paintings, dance, poetry - something modern shops communicate to you, now might be the time to channel your grief via them.

Purge all the extreme feelings into your magazine. Sing your coronary coronary heart out to cathartic breakup songs till you ache with remedy. Paint the raging chaos indoors you in formidable, honest strokes.

Tap into the collective focus of diverse artists and creators who've walked this route in advance than you. Their songs, art work, writing screen how conventional heartbreak is. You experience less on my own knowing others have made it through to the opportunity element too.

Making artwork reconnects you collectively with your spirit. You rediscover splendor and which means that. When phrases fail, the soul though yearns to specific itself through creativity. Let it go along with the waft abundantly.

Get Moving

As lethargy and exhaustion set in, getting your body transferring will become critical. Emotions trapped in muscles tighten into tension, weighing you down. A slow body mirrors the stuck, lifelessness of depression.

Combat the emptiness with simple exercise - drift on useful walks often, spend money on home workout movement photographs. Cleaning and organizing your living area can provide emotional launch thru bodily hobby too.

Yoga specifically permits loosen up clenched muscle companies and circulate stagnant electricity. Release negativity at the exhale, while inhaling staying electricity and perseverance. Effort restores a feel of empowerment.

Moving in advance physical, little by little, motivates you to maintain progressing emotionally too. Each step effects in some different till you find out your stride yet again.

Let Nature Nurture You

Mother Nature's recovery balm soothes the soul whilst you're hurting. Spending time outside, mainly around water, lifts your vibrations while you're feeling low.

Stroll through a peaceful garden, sit down below the shade of a generous tree, wander along the ocean coastline. Absorb the gradual, grounding rhythm of the herbal worldwide all round you.

Tune your senses to the swaying grass, rustling leaves, creating a music birds. Feel the sun kissing your pores and skin, the breeze kissing your face. Nature harmonizes your fragmented electricity lower returned into wholeness. It returns you to equanimity with endless persistence.

Escape the claustrophobic partitions of gloom and breathe deeply once more in nature's nurturing tranquility. The earth allows you till you can stand regular to your very own yet again.

Surrender the Fantasy

The aspect about grief is that, at times, it temptingly tugs you backwards in vicinity of forwards. You start rationalizing motives to hold to faux hopes.

You glorify the best instances at the equal time as blatantly denying the crimson flags. Your thoughts plays suggestions on you, convincing you they may come once more if you simply wait it out. You become lost in fable, paralyzed in emotional quicksand.

When this happens, you consciously reaffirm your dedication to surrendering the delusion and shifting on. As painful as it's far, you admit to yourself that this courting can't be revived. All the wishing within the worldwide gained't trade what is.

Once you completely surrender, grieving follows its natural route. Energy spent resisting the brand new truth transforms into energy spent growing a present day existence. Loss clears location for better want to discover you when the time is proper.

Feel It All, Then Let It Go

In many methods the departure of affection is similar to the departure of a loved one. Grief is the price we pay for bold to care deeply. Only time and tears wipe the slate easy.

You clearly revel in all of it - every wave of suffering, loneliness, anger, remorse. But a few element magical takes region whilst you give up resisting the grief. You permit the river drift freely thru you, records you can't save you its herbal movement.

In allowing the swell of feelings their whole expression with out judgement or limit, they loosen their grip on you grade by grade. Like hurricane clouds they acquire, unharness their downpour, then in the end dissipate.

Grief transforms into remembrance. The extra you permit yourself to revel in, the greater your coronary coronary heart opens as a great deal as delight and ardour all over again. From the compost of loss, new increase blooms. You lightly release the past to live, laugh, and love freely in the gift over again.

Rise Like the Phoenix

In historic mythologies, the phoenix represented death accompanied with the useful resource of the usage of rebirth thru fireplace. This legendary bird bursts into flame in its nest, most effective to upward thrust majestically from the ashes once more.

Like the phoenix, you allow the purifying fires of grief refine and resurrect you. You give up the phantasm of manage over a situation which have become in the long run past your electricity. And thru the darkness, your slight shines on.

You honor the important mourning, understanding it empowers the renewal organized to spread. From the ashes of what is lengthy long gone, you resurrect your spirit and chart an impressive new route.

With grace and grit, you start rebuilding your life. Stone via stone, you erect a destiny very well your non-public. Here sorrow softens into satisfaction, expertise emerges from wounds, and your maximum proper self awakens.

Rise, phoenix. Spread your splendid wings another time. The ashes have fertilized the soil to your most terrific rebirth.

## Chapter 3: Practicing Self-Care And Self-Compassion

Curled up on the sofa under a mountain of blankets, you mindlessly scroll social media for the hundredth time nowadays. Crumpled tissues clutter the espresso desk. Your hair is a knotted mess, and you can not maintain in thoughts the remaining time you showered or ate a right meal.

In this pit of depression, taking care of your self proper now seems next to impossible. You have in reality no electricity or motivation. The smallest mission seems like mountain climbing Mt. Everest. Besides, a voice inner asks, why hassle whilst you feel so nugatory and damaged?

But now extra than ever, nurturing your self with compassion is vital for recuperation. Think of it this manner - if your terrific buddy changed into going through a painful breakup, you will rush to their side with love and care, proper? So be definitely as gentle with yourself on this hard time.

## Start with the Basics

In survival mode, self-care falls via the usage of the wayside. The fundamentals like dozing, ingesting, bathing get overlooked at the same time as depression sinks in. But stabilizing your foundations another time is the first step in rebuilding.

Commit to a normal sleep ordinary, even in case you need to depend upon treatment quickly. Fill your refrigerator with glowing, nourishing elements. Shower each day and located on actual garments, not simply pajamas. Drink masses of water and take nutrients.

When you're jogging on empty, emotions without trouble spiral out of control. Mastering the fundamentals gives stability so that you can begin processing grief from a extra grounded region.

## Let Others Hold You Up

Vulnerability is hard when you're used to being sturdy and self-enough. But the beauty of relationships is that others can in short convey you if you have no electricity left.

Silently offer a chum your hand, tears streaming down your face, and let them preserve you as you sooner or later launch the damage. Accept a domestic-cooked meal from family, even if you have no appetite. Receive gratitude even as cherished ones assist you to understand how an awful lot they cherish having you of their lives.

Humans are harassed out for network and connection. You don't have to - nor need to you - stroll this street by myself. Let folks who surely care assist undergo the burden in little techniques.

Move Your Body

Physical motion is remedy. It releases sense-particular endorphins and neurochemicals that boost your mood. Even a quick walk throughout the block can get your blood flowing.

Stretch out the tears until your body feels lighter. Put on song and permit your frame to bop out the grief till you smile and sweat. Develop an exercise habitual that turns into your only self-care ritual.

When emotional pain feels countless, the frame gives us a way out - through mild movement, one step and one breath at a time. Keep putting one foot within the the front of the alternative.

Commit to Your Healing

To truly flip the corner, dedicate ordinary time to your healing. Treat your self kindly, as you may a near friend. Make a list of things that spark pleasure and cause.

Perhaps you sign up for that pottery magnificence you've been seeking to take. You undertake a puppy to fill the lonely regions. You hike in nature every weekend, volunteer at a steady haven, or be part of a help organisation.

Whatever will boom your spirits, prioritize it. Your days become centered spherical self-discovery in preference to wallowing. You find your stride another time thru walking bravely.

## Forgive Your Setbacks

Some days the development feels so promising. Other days the accidents enjoy as uncooked because of the fact the day they first opened. There isn't always any linear timeline to recuperation.

When you backslide into doubt, depression, even attaining out on your ex, have compassion for yourself. Forgive the setbacks and hold shifting earlier. Progress ebbs and flows like the ocean's waves.

The adventure is never smooth, but you're in no manner alone. Even the most painful stumbles alongside the way form you into someone with extra grit, empathy and resilience. All of it is building your courage muscle groups.

## Detox Your Space

External surroundings powerfully effect internal states. A chaotic, gloomy location mirrors and magnifies unhappiness. But de-cluttering your residing environment feels like de-cluttering your mind.

Box up vintage pics, offers and mementos that evoke obsessive nostalgia or remorse. Re-installation furnishings to create a sparkling go together with the glide. Display art work, candles and vegetation that nourish your spirit. Let greater slight and air flow into.

When your private area reflects renewal, positivity and comfort, your thoughts certainly align. Outside order catalyzes internal order. Your home turns into a sanctuary over again.

Unplug from Technology

Facebook invites pointless social comparisons. Instagram idealizes everybody else's lives. Online stalking your ex handiest reopens wounds. The net often hurts greater than enables located up-breakup.

Limit social media and senseless browsing. Instead nourish your self with unique sports that have interaction your senses. Take an enriching splendor, get lost in an engrossing e-book, prepare dinner or bake some trouble comforting.

Unplugging from technology forces you inward to mirror. The static noise of consistent distraction gets changed through calm presence. Healing springs from mindfulness, now not multimedia.

Reframe Your Thoughts

Almost robotically, your internal critic emerges accountable you for the breakup. "You're now not quite enough, clever enough, cute sufficient" it publicizes. Left unchecked, self-judgment maintains you caught.

Catch the ones thoughts like passing clouds. Replace harsh judgments with gentler perspectives. Would you talk this manner to someone you want dearly? If not, why permit it within yourself?

Treat yourself with the kindness and understanding you deserve. Write down empowering mantras and your notable trends. You aren't described via this loss. Your inherent clearly worth stays intact.

Surrender the Outcome

The mind likes to strategize the manner to win your ex decrease returned through complex ploys. Or it swings the opportunity way - catastrophizing that you'll come to be by myself all the time not able to love or get hold of as right with once more.

Neither excessive is rooted in fact. Let bypass of seeking to control uncontrollable outcomes. All your electricity goes into considerate motion these days, surrendering the unknowable future.

Making peace with uncertainty is difficult however liberating. You advantage superb electricity at the same time as you prevent trying truth to enjoy solid or happy. Uncertainty way some aspect is possible.

## Keep the Faith

Some days will deliver doubt, darkness, hopelessness. On these days, your quality technique is to hold the religion. Faith that the storm will skip. Faith in your resilience. Faith that love and pleasure wait down the road.

When you can't see the light on the prevent of the tunnel, permit your inner moderate guide you one step at a time. If you can't trust in yourself, lean on the electricity of loved ones who receive as actual with in you.

Keep walking. Keep letting pass a chunk more each day. Keep envisioning the man or woman you're becoming. And never prevent trusting that the sun will upward thrust all all over again.

## Seeing Your Ex Realistically

Looking again, all you keep in mind are the coolest times. That romantic weekend getaway, how they surprised you with plants at artwork, the manner they held you on lazy Sunday mornings.

Seen through rose-coloured glasses, your ex seems first-rate. Your thoughts convinces you they have been your soulmate, which you'll in no way discover love like that once more. Maybe if you had absolutely attempted greater difficult, they'd nevertheless be proper proper right here.

But painful as it's far, you need to do away with the rose-coloured glasses. This idealized model of your ex now not represents truth. A easy-eyed view in their flaws and the relationship's problems is vital for moving on.

Get Distance and Perspective

Raw emotions make objective perception nearly no longer feasible proper after a breakup. Your grief magnifies the positives and explains away the negatives. Healthy distance presents perspective.

Cut touch definitely so your feelings can detach and thoughts clarify. Fill some time with sports that empower you. Make plans with fantastic friends who see your well worth. Traveling also expands your point of view.

Gradually, place lets in you to look the connection dynamics more as it need to be. You apprehend processes you compartmentalized purple flags or placated horrible behaviors. Distance reveals what you grew to emerge as a blind eye to.

Inventory the Red Flags

With new mindset, make an real listing of your ex's horrible tendencies and behaviors. Document patterns that need to have given you pause from the begin.

Did they often positioned you down or forget about approximately approximately your emotions? Did they've got trouble committing or continuously appear to shy away? Were they controlling or short to anger? Did they drink too much or have interaction in first-rate dangerous behavior?

Don't censor or sugarcoat this stock. However lengthy the list, understand that you glossed over those failings while you have got been although with them, no longer because the issues didn't exist. But now you be aware truely.

Ask Why It Ended

The thoughts craves closure. Rehash the relationship's death with a counselor or impartial pals. Seek honest insights into problems you'll possibly were unaware of.

Were your lengthy-term values in the end misaligned? Did the relationship end up one-sided or stagnant? Did dishonesty, disloyalty or deal-breaking variations erode its foundations?

Answering why it ended allows redirect disappointment into records. Heartbreak most effective makes enjoy at the same time as you notice the affection definitely for what it have turn out to be. With truth comes the power to allow pass and pass ahead.

## Recall the Bad Times

When nostalgia gadgets in, intentionally convey to thoughts recollections of the relationship at its worst. Revisiting painful moments with readability maintains subjects in mindset.

Remember the terrible combat in which hurtful subjects have been stated. Recall how small and insecure they made you revel in. See the instances they promised to trade but will assist you to down. Feel how chronic frustration and absence of agree with seeped in.

The horrific times provide evidence that this relationship changed into a long way from great. Through remembering its darker realities, the illusion of your ex's perfection in the long run shatters.

## Accept Their Flaws

Without placing your ex on a pedestal, you may exercising recognition. Accept that they have been now not a few best soulmate without flaws - they were truely human. Fallible, complicated, inconsistent like we all are.

You can contemplate their problems with empathy in preference to judgment. Accepting their imperfections lets in your forgiveness, compassion, and in the end letting go. The tons much less resentment you harbor, the lighter your spirit feels.

Pity, anger nor denial changes what became. Radical beauty of the reality is the route beforehand. This clears region for modern-day love based totally on honesty.

See How You Changed Too

This manner is not approximately villainizing your ex each. With clean eyes, reflect on how you may have contributed to troubles in the courting too.

## Chapter 4: Letting Go Of Reminders And Mementos

Just whilst you count on your coping with the breakup k, it hits you all once more. You're blindsided by means of way of grief washing over you out of nowhere.

Then you apprehend - it modified into the antique sweater they left at the back of that brought about it. The love letters tucked away in a subject. The voicemails you in reality can't erase but.

Your residing environment is full of painful reminders that keep reopening wounds. A clean destroy way a literal easy-out of mementos and property imbued with emotional power from the relationship. This cleaning ritual marks a pivotal shift proper into a modern-day bankruptcy.

Be Brutally Honest

Go via your area with brutal honesty. Gather up each belonging, card, photo, playlist, social media submit, present - something that ties your coronary heart and thoughts to the past. Avoid sugarcoating or clinging to keepsakes for flimsy reasons.

Stuffed animals, mixtapes, interior jokes - even sweet devices spark unhappiness now. The more ruthless you are, the greater lightness you'll experience. Packing up the evidence of shared records lifts an first rate weight.

Tune Into Your Emotions

Notice how each memento you manage makes you revel in as you type through. Angry? Wistful? Sentimental? Nostalgic? Heartbroken? This emotional test-in manner allows detach.

Some gadgets you'll with out troubles detail with, others you'll struggle over. When hesitation units in, sit down with the feeling in advance than finding out. Treat your self lightly thru this touchy purging manner.

Create a Memory Box

For devices you can't but relinquish, location them in a decorative area. Select huge keepsakes like tour pictures or handwritten letters.

Seal this memory container up for storage in preference to leaving reminders strewn round your house. When sufficient time passes, it's far going to be much less tough to revisit the contents extra objectively and sort all over again. For now, honoring symbols of what you shared with out clinging is a healthy stability.

Trash, Donate, or Return Items

Next comes the freeing element - getting rid of things in reality. Pour your progressive strength into the manner you launch them based on the this means that they carry approximately.

Trash less highly-priced gifts or unique replaceable items. Donate assets in authentic state of affairs to charity. Return greater treasured or sentimental gadgets at once for your ex as a manner to't linger like ghosts.

However you pick out to purge, embody this ritual as an act of letting pass on the bodily aircraft to reflect emotional launch.

Do a Deep Cleanse

Simply clearing out doesn't guarantee remnants of their energy don't linger. After getting rid of your ex's property, do a deeper lively cleanse.

Open domestic domestic home windows to flow into sparkling air and mild. Smudge your property with cleaning sage or palo santo. Vacuum away stagnant power.Clean each room and floor thoroughly. Envision your sacred location becoming awesome and uplifting.

You must experience palpably lighter. If emotional heaviness clings, keep purifying your environment till your house appears like a calming sanctuary once more.

Rearrange and Redecorate

With your ex's presence energetically cleared, rearrange fixtures to create a today's go along with the flow. Switch round decor to reflect your non-public fashion. Display inspiring prices, art work, pix of loved ones who enhance you up.

Makeover your mattress room to mention it as your very non-public sacred sleep vicinity another time. Update bedding, add flowers, create a dreamy vibe. When your personal surroundings feels reclaimed and refreshed, your whole outlook shifts.

Release Digital Memories

Virtual areas require a cleanse too. Digital communique makes deleting memories trickier than burning vintage love letters. Resist the temptation to reread texts or social media posts for emotional self-torture.

Archive or delete texts, photographs, playlists that tempt painful reminiscing. Remove or block them on all social media so digital reminders not capture you off shield. Free your era existence from the ghostly energy of the beyond.

Reclaim Special Songs

Music often holds a number of the exceptional reminiscences. A track that felt magical while you shared it collectively along with your ex all at once stings with sadness. But tune's splendor belongs to you, now not really one man or woman.

Gradually start reclaiming songs that speak to your spirit by way of the use of rediscovering what you like approximately them - the usage of with the home home windows down creating a tune each word, dancing spherical your room with carefree abandon, or collapsing into nostalgic tears because it's in order that rattling stunning.

Let them expand your life another time, in area of constricting it.

Embrace Closure

This clearing gadget seals up the past, developing place for the destiny. Out with the antique, in with the trendy. What as quickly as carried meaning serves no reason anymore besides preserving you another time.

Trust in the cleansing energy of launch. Each souvenir you free yourself from lightens your load a chunk extra. These moves mirror internal intentions breaking unfastened from grief's gravity.

The extra thoroughly you cleanse the slate, the quicker peace and closure settle into the empty areas. You're organized for something comes subsequent without remnants from the day past weighting you down.

See Each Letting Go as an Act of Self-Love

Treat this transition amongst chapters for your existence gently and meaningfully. Even if you falter or 2d-bet along the way, stay devoted for your course of release.

Each souvenir you shred, delete, donate, trash or container up is in the end an act of honoring your self - your growth, your resilience, your readiness for pleasure.

Keep surrendering the past until your environment certainly reflect your spirit over again. You deserve an environment as mild, whole and relatively yours as your future now can be.

Reconnecting with Old Hobbies and Passions

The courting occupied numerous your power and identification. You orientated your whole existence round your companion. Now you enjoy empty, like a leaf disconnected from any sense of cause. Who are you with out them?

But this area after loss invitations profound self-rediscovery. You get reacquainted with dormant pursuits and passions. It's time to reignite the pursuits and sports sports that mild you up from within, bringing you joy and because of this over again.

Let your internal spirit manual you organically closer to what nourishes you maximum. By following what calls you, forgotten components of yourself flourish all over again to existence.

Remember Your Enthusiasms

Make a list of interests, hobbies and responsibilities you've omitted however despite the fact that make your eyes sparkle. Get nostalgic thinking lower back on what excited you earlier than this dating.

Perhaps you done guitar in a band, hiked each weekend, dreamed of taking off your very very own bakery in the long run. Reconnect with the sports that fed your soul, no longer due to the reality someone else desired you to enjoy them but due to the truth they contemplated you.

Release Guilt

Guilt occasionally creeps up as you shift popularity again to your self. Feelings of selfishness or irresponsibility echo beyond voices of judgment and criticism.

But following your joys is the opposite of selfish - it's self-whole. Nurturing your pastimes permits you to nurture others from a place of abundance in choice to lack. Don't allow fake guilt sabotage your increase.

Explore and Experiment

Next comes the amusing detail - exploring and experimenting until you rediscover what clicks. Sign up for training that pique your interest, like painting, pottery, improv comedy, or wine tasting.

Join a membership or community targeted around hobbies you want to investigate greater about, like hiking, ebook discussions, cooking, or volunteering. Tinker and play with long-unnoticed instruments, crafts, or sports tool accumulating dust within the garage.

See what sparks childlike enthusiasm once you immerse yourself genuinely. Follow every whim with large-eyed surprise to locate the treasures interior.

Schedule Your Passions

At first getting reacquainted together with your passions may additionally feel extraordinary or uncertain. The way to combine them into your existence another time is through scheduling everyday time for them.

Add your private pastimes into your each day or weekly calendar similar to you may different critical commitments. Honor this time with your self as sacred space to rediscover your joys, free from the pull of various responsibilities.

Start small if wished - 15 mins or 1/2 of an hour devoted on your crafts, instrument, yoga exercise or a few thing fills you up. Then little by little boom time spent doing what devices your spirit hovering.

Create With Abandon

Instead of harsh self-grievance, deliver your self whole innovative freedom to play without demanding approximately very last outcomes.

Art and music do no longer want to be perfect or polished.

Give watercolors a remarkable splash or wake a guitar from its silence with a few rusty chords. Scribble freely on your journal or tinker in the kitchen just for the pride of making some component along side your palms.

You might also additionally wonder your self what emerges while you create in fact for the satisfaction of feeling self-expressed and alive. Let suggestion lead with the innocence of a child complete of considerable-eyed wonder.

Find Your Community

Happiness in no way arises in isolation, only via connection. Find your those who percent commonplace passions so you can nerd out together.

Join a entertainment sports sports business enterprise, hiking institution, ebook membership or volunteer software program to surround yourself with uplifting souls who recognize the sports you understand. Share in the laughter, help and feel of belonging.

Your vibe draws your tribe. When you lead together at the side of your real hobbies, you genuinely draw others with comparable enthusiasms into your orbit actually with the resource of being your self.

Uplevel and Set Goals

After reestablishing a regular exercise, start setting desires to undertaking your self further. Uplevel your talents and statistics round your interest or hobby location to complement it.

Take better stage commands, attend lectures or trainings, join a mentorship institution. Set timelines for completing projects. Enter contests to encourage excellence. Say positive to opportunities for increase as your passions flower into a larger a part of your existence.

Alignment Attracts Abundance

In the vacancy following a breakup, coming across what fulfills you offers your days renewed meaning. Passions summon your spirit at the same time as it feels deflated. They fill voids with purpose and energy from the interior out.

By revisiting antique interests and gaining expertise of recent capabilities, lengthy-dormant dreams awaken. Possibilities display themselves even as you follow idea anywhere it leads you. Curiosity flows freely another time.

Your destiny unfolds truly on the equal time as you live in alignment collectively together with your truest joys. Passion breeds abundance. What seems like play will become sacred artwork. Your existence overflowing with enthusiasm attracts its most manifestation.

## Chapter 5: Trying New Things And Meeting New People

Stepping out of your consolation sector while you're already feeling damage or insecure can sound unappealing. You crave the acquainted to appease your wounds in difficult instances. But hiding away breeds loneliness and stagnation.

Instead, now may be the correct moment to courageously amplify your horizons. Say yes to novel critiques that jolt you out of ruts. Meet people out of doors your regular circles who growth attitude.

Through embracing the unusual, you rediscover your adventurous spirit. Curiosity throws open domestic home windows and doors prolonged near. You keep in mind how exciting it feels to broaden, evolve and discover anew.

Face Small Fears First

When trying new subjects, start with small fears to construct self assurance in your self.

Sign up for that dance, improv or karaoke elegance you have got generally decided interesting. Dine at an person eating place providing spicy cuisine you've in no way tasted in advance than.

Introduce yourself to buddies you've visible round but in no way spoken to. Ask someone on a date after changing glances on the coffee store. Volunteer at an unusual fitness medical institution or homeless safe haven for your network.

As you get snug venturing out of doors consolation zones in chunk-sized ways, your courage muscle strengthens for even large horizons to spread.

Book Exciting Excursions

Nothing expands horizons greater than travelling somewhere actually new, whether or not or not or not on my own or with friends. Explore a city you've usually desired to go to, or pick out a far off holiday spot that guarantees stunning surroundings and out of doors adventure.

If price range restrict tremendous excursion, examine close by locations you may get away to for handiest a weekend. Go camping, wine tasting, retreat website hosting, something to stir idea and surprise thru serendipitous publicity to the unusual.

Immerse yourself completely within the nearby way of existence. Meet fellow tourists in hostels and on excursions. Let the pride of discovery peel your spirit large open.

Venture Off the Beaten Path

When you tour, withstand the temptation of overly-deliberate itineraries and tourist traps. Wandering offers space for unexpected delights and reviews.

Mosey via colorful facet streets that department off busy avenues. Pop into hollow-in-the-wall cafes and stores in choice to large chains. Strike up conversations with the first-rate locals you come across.

Adventure necessarily exhibits the open coronary heart. By veering off the beaten route, you come upon hidden gems no guidebook need to ever map out. Follow your interest like a winding direction through the barren region of the arena.

Learn Exciting New Skills

Trying new subjects can also surely advise growing your capability set. Spark self-discovery with the useful resource of learning capabilities out of doors your facts and historical past - a few factor that activates part of yourself lying dormant.

Take a bread making or photographs elegance. Learn a way to rock climb, surf, ballroom dance or communicate Italian. Volunteer to help construct houses for those in want or help in plants and fauna conservation efforts.

Mastering novel capabilities boosts self perception. You discover entire new dimensions of who you're and what you're capable of through palms-on research.

Meet People Who Intrigue You

Part of widening horizons approach increasing social circles too. Seek out people whose perspectives, talents, careers or life extend your angle.

Introduce yourself to artists painting on the park, the tech CEO giving a lecture, or fellow volunteers at a full-size charity occasion. Learn from the ones following unconventional paths with admirable authenticity.

Diverse organisation stressful situations you. Witnessing humans living boldly evokes you to shed limitations imposed through way of way of fear or conformity. The right connections wake up dormant opportunities interior your self.

Say Yes to Invitations

Often the intuition after a breakup is isolation and withdrawal from social sports. But right now your spirit goals community, newness and pleasure. Combat melancholy thru pronouncing sure.

Accept invitations even if you feel some hesitation. Go to the birthday dinner, wedding ceremony, live performance, outside barbeque or paintings glad hour you may usually skip.

Approach every event with an open thoughts. You in no way recognize who you may meet or what possibilities also can spread through stepping outdoor old routines into glowing areas glowing with potential.

Don't Take Rejection Personally

Expanding your world way taking greater social, professional or romantic dangers. Sometimes new people will reciprocate your openness. But rejection usually takes region too.

When someone declines an invite or expresses disinterest, do not take it as purpose for hurt or self-blame. It actually manner your paths have been not meant to intersect at this juncture. Keep smiling and in search of kindred spirits.

Maintain attitude on the equal time as confronted with rejection. Let it roll off your again and hold coronary heart open for the connections which can be destined to enhance your existence significantly up earlier.

Chart Your Own Course

Stepping outside consolation zones can enjoy intimidating at the start. But the more you make bigger horizons and embody unexpected research, the greater readability and self warranty you advantage about charting your non-public path.

Trying new subjects teaches you that happiness comes from inner, no longer outside situations. Your internal moderate shines brightly at the identical time as you observe your curiosity into unexplored terrain, irrespective of tour spot.

Growth is predicated upon now not on reality, but the braveness to take formidable leaps of religion within the course of instances of uncertainty. Saying high-quality throws open windows of opportunities so your future can find you. Keep growing.

Forgive and Forget:

Moving Past Anger and Bitterness

In the turbulent aftermath of heartbreak, anger and bitterness creep in like undesirable houseguests. Once invited internal, they overstay their welcome - lounging spherical, feet for your espresso desk, trash piled up. Evicting them will become tough.

But clinging to resentment poisons your thoughts, body and spirit. It maintains you trapped as a sufferer, fingers clenched round ache from the unchangeable beyond. To flow into ahead, you have to open your fingers - forgiving your ex, the situation, and most significantly your self.

Feel the Anger, But Don't Feed It

Anger merits acknowledgement, now not suppression. Let your self vent frustrations into your magazine or with close to confidants. Yell right into a pillow if it presents emotional release. Anger expressed constructively disarms its electricity.

But pay attention limitless rumination that feeds resentment like kindling on a fireplace. Constantly rehashing your ex's transgressions with angry bitterness winds up burning you. Anger, allowed to smolder unchecked, scalds your peace and distorts truth.

Get Curious About the Cause

Explore the roots feeding your anger with out judgement. Are you more harm over perceived betrayals and flaws? Disappointed the fantasy didn't in form reality? Ashamed you didn't save you the very last results? Afraid of being on my own or in no way locating better?

Understanding anger's center wounds opens area for recovery. Approach these hurts like a curios detective or compassionate counselor searching for to understand in advance than advising. Shine mild in place of cursing the darkness.

Write a Forgiveness Letter

Writing out your conflicts, disappointments and pains in letter form frequently softens anger's sharp edges. This gadget externalizes inner turmoil, organizing a jumble of emotions into easy phrases.

Write as even though immediately addressing your ex - uncensored but not cruelty. Describe how they harm you, however additionally your element in hurts. Admit procedures you projected unrealistic expectations onto them. Ultimately choice them well, liberating them lightly.

The letter can remain non-public. Simply formulating grievances into smooth sentences releases their grip. Forgiveness flows definitely even as you shift angle from blame to humanity.

## Set Healthy Boundaries

Anger from time to time stems lots less from the beyond than worry of ongoing boundary violations. If contact continues permitting harm, defend your peace with organization barriers or distance.

Kindly however unequivocally specific behaviors you can no longer tolerate, if any further dating is to exist. If amends are refused, permit skip knowing you communicated your fact. Allow herbal effects to educate what your phrases couldn't.

Creating safety to technique anger aside from its deliver empowers you. Boundaries align words and actions, freeing you from mistreatment's vicious cycle.

## Rewrite the Story

In your mind, recast the relationship's narrative from victimhood to increase. See it as a difficult but crucial step in your unique path, not a meaningless waste.

What existence training did this chapter educate you about yourself, relationships, discernment, braveness? How did you end up wiser, stronger, more compassionate and affected individual? What traits did you discover receiving love located out to you?

An empowering internal story transforms anger to gratitude. Every revel in - even painful ones - expands your capacity for knowledge and pleasure whilst reframed as items revealing your wholeness.

Find Cathartic Release

Anger alchemizes into extraordinary strength whilst you channel it into effective stores. Physical hobby, creativity and network provide healthful cathartic launch.

Run or dance to energetic music until you sweat out toxicity. Write a inform-all music or paint formidable summary paintings to unharness internal chaos. Join a guide organization to percent brazenly in a judgment-loose location.

Convert fiery emotions into powerful gas uplifting your self and others. What emerges is purified and useful - molten anger cast into courageous compassion.

Send Love from Afar

Once you technique the anger, begin sending love. In your thoughts's eye, preference your ex nicely on their private growth adventure. See them as fallacious however sacred souls collectively with you, traversing this difficult human enjoy as extraordinary they're capable of.

Pray for his or her restoration and happiness. Hold them in the mild mild of information. Bless all they have got taught you, and forgive all they couldn't provide. Send gratitude for the methods your lives touched, no matter the truth that chapters forestall.

Bitterness can't coexist with the goal of affection. Distance your coronary heart from beyond pains through boundless goodwill on your ex's highest unfoldment.

## Accept What You Can't Control

Ultimately, placing onto resentment trying to strain atonement or apology only hurts you. You can't manipulate your ex's alternatives or flaws. But you could manipulate letting bypass of idealized expectancies that breed resentments.

Accept that closure may also moreover moreover remain elusive. Make peace that amends also can never come. Yet nonetheless stroll beforehand with openness. Allow your ex their very very own imperfect path, smash free yours, with compassion.

All you may manage is your self - your responses, reactions and readiness to get maintain of the education with grace. What effective freedom this brings.

## Chapter 6: Envisioning Your Fresh Start

The rearview reflect shows a landscape affected by painful relics - recollections, regrets, dashed goals for a future now canceled. But residing on the dwindled surroundings in the back of your best steers life off route.

To skip beyond the pain of the day before today, reputation completely on the big open street in advance instead. Adjust the mirror to reflect truly enough of the past to guide you - then set your points of hobby on glowing visions emerging over the horizon.

The power lies not in the wreckage you've left in the back of, but the hopeful excursion spot your compass now points in the path of.

Define Your Dreams

Envisioning your fullest capability begins offevolved thru way of getting smooth to your desires. Revisit antique bucket lists or mag approximately desires that extend your spirit.

Do you aspire to excursion the world, start your very personal corporation, draw near a talent? Return to high school, relocate, volunteer? Who do you want to become and the manner? Outline concrete steps to make goals actual.

Align actions with aspirations. When your day by day life indicates your goals, you occur them into truth. Make vision forums or schedules to anchor creativeness into regular.

Set Short-Term Goals

In addition to large goals, set brief-term desires to maintain momentum. Small accomplishments construct yourself assurance to hold development amongst wider milestones.

Achievable goals would possibly encompass normal health club instructions, restricting nightly wine to weekends, signing up for a class, calling a pal as quickly as each week, or saving a sure amount financially. Check off each intention as you whole it.

Little through the use of little, imaginative and prescient actualizes thru diligence. Daily disciplines cultivate the person that will sooner or later satisfy your maximum goals. Keep stepping ahead.

Do What Scares You

Often the bravest desires push you out of doors comfort zones, that might to start with initiate fear and resistance. Let formidable dreams extend in area of lessen who you're.

Maybe deep down you long to sing on level, begin a nonprofit, emerge as a pilot, stay overseas. Rather than dismissing such desires as unrealistic, lean in. Gather records, connect to mentors, face fears head-on understanding increase lives outdoor obstacles.

Your destiny unveils itself at the same time as you are taking the jump. What feels scary nowadays empowers you the next day. Through courage, you increase wings.

Surround Yourself with Optimists

Curate your community deliberately via spending time with brilliant, supportive those who recall for your capability. Their buoyant electricity lifts you higher.

Share your goals and development freely. Let their encouragements drown out internal doubts. They cheer you on as you are taking dangers, chasing visions no longer however made real.

Hope can feel elusive by myself, however multiplies interior inspiring agency. Their religion replenishes your religion whilst you sense depleted. Envision together.

Trust the Unknown

Plotting the path earlier brings consolation. But over-attachment to plans limits possibilities. Learn to include uncertainty as part of the adventure.

Release the reins of searching for to manipulate exactly how your vision unfolds. Make room for satisfactory detours and unexpected advantages. Trust in lifestyles's unfolding despite the fact that the holiday spot remains dubious.

Your purpose isn't always to force outcomes, but to expose up in fact these days. Each 2nd seeds the following. By walking with faith, doorways open you in no way imagined.

Emit a Positive Frequency

To entice your desires into reality, broadcast their frequencies thru idea, word and deed.

Spend time visualizing your fulfilled visions vividly, inhabiting every detail together along with your senses. Speak affirmations aloud like "I am brave" or "My gadgets are identified." Take bold movement, no matter how small, that moves you inside the path of your objectives.

Energetic and practical efforts align to draw future to you. Dare to assert your worthiness to gain all you preference. The universe responds in type on your music.

Practice Gratitude

Some days persevering with the uphill journey feels laborious. Reconnect with suggestion thru gratitude. Give thanks for fitness, loved ones, functions and for all the development made up to now.

Count blessings for the breath to your lungs, the schooling that opened your thoughts, the privilege of dwelling in a safe u.S.A.. Appreciate your blessings and strengths. Gratitude makes steep roads less tough to climb with attitude.

When gratitude fills your coronary heart every day, shortage can not take root there. Abundance blooms within the fertile soil of appreciation. See it already gift indoors and spherical you.

Stay Open and Flexible

Remain open and bendy to course corrections as you actualize your visions. Evolving situations require adapting plans at the same time as staying actual to middle longings.

Not each mile will unfold easily. Expect bumps alongside the way. But with resilience and creativity, you steer lower again inside the path of goals that enjoy like future. With flexibility, no impediment completely bars you.

Your purpose isn't always any single very last effects, however the braveness to stay clearly. Wherever the journey leads, encompass it as part of your becoming.

Love Yourself First:

Learning To Be Happy Alone

The empty region left within the once more of after a breakup can tempt you to hurry into the arms of someone new to keep away from feeling lonely. But this short restore frequently effects in repeating antique patterns in new packages.

True restoration first requires mastering to feel complete to your very own. Instead of desperately in search of each other to finish you, make bigger an unconditional dating with yourself.

By pouring your power into self-care, boom and pleasure, you rebuild self-don't forget and self-love from within. Your internal moderate turns into so exciting that a few other individual truly enhances in choice to defines your happiness.

Date Yourself

Romance yourself with considerate gestures that say "I love you for precisely who you are." Plan solo dates doing activities that enliven your spirit and heighten self-popularity.

Savor that museum display off, hike thru suitable nature, or live performance with preferred music. Explore new eating places, schooling, stores. Dress as much as exit dancing, decide to a spa day, toast for your fitness and strengths.

Through self-care and a laugh, reconnect together along with your passions and abilties. Fall in love with existence once more from the inner out. You are the accomplice your coronary heart has been looking ahead to.

## Overcome Aloneness

Solitude can also initially revel in uncomfortable after losing an intimate relationship. Lean into this problem in region of distracting from it superficially.

Sit with yourself in a few unspecified time within the future of quiet meditations. Purposely spend an midnight cellular phone-unfastened. Go to that movie or cafe on my own. Feel the aloneness certainly, embracing your private real agency.

Getting comfortable on my own reveals loneliness as an phantasm. You come to recognize you're already complete and entire, now not a fragment desiring very last touch. Aloneness ceases being a trouble searching solving.

## Set Healthy Boundaries

Evaluate relationships with honesty to look which burn up in choice to top off you. Then set less assailable limitations spherical time and strength given.

Limit touch with crucial, judgmental humans. Politely decline invitations that don't uplift. Take area from manipulative or clingy connections. Prioritize your needs unapologetically.

You honor others super by using using the usage of nurturing wholeness within first. Draw clean lines so you can supply from abundance in preference to lack. Mutually supportive relationships blossom on the equal time as you have a tendency your garden nicely.

Embrace Imperfection

Perfectionism erodes self confidence, as you constantly criticize yourself for failing to fulfill unrealistic necessities. Combat inner grievance with radical self-popularity rather.

Love yourself for the messy, quirky, flawlessly imperfect man or woman you're. Allow humor, humility and compassion closer to your very very very own flaws. Talk to your self as a worrying friend may also, with slight honesty free of judgment.

You are well worth now not due to the fact you are best, however because of the reality you are human. You have everything you want within to be at peace simply as you are. Wholeness embraces all.

Take Creative Risks

Expressing your proper self builds courage and pleasure from within. Take modern risks that introduce you for your tremendous functionality.

Sing wildly within the bathe, write uncensored poetry, photo nature's beauty, paint precis art work. Play guitar or cook dinner dinner simplest for yourself, with out disturbing what others will suppose.

Through unfiltered self-expression, you fall in love along side your originality. Boldly dreaming and making keeps your internal spark critical. Don't hide your slight away ever once more.

Embrace Your Sensuality

Reconnect at the facet of your sensual facet through dance, aromatherapy, highly-priced fabric, baths, movement. Revel in sensations that kindle your colourful aliveness.

Sensuality is not about attempting to find validation externally. It springs from delighting for your very very own radiant embodiment, your way of uniquely being inside the worldwide.

When you particular sensuality with unapologetic freedom, you reclaim your wholeness. Your spirit stays illuminated from inside, no matter what unfolds externally.

Find Fulfillment In Small Joys

Learn to find happiness in simplicity - cooking food, studying books, taking walks outdoor. Take more fulfillment in lifestyles's subtle beauty disregarded in advance than.

Savor your morning espresso slowly. Pause to take in a sunset's colorings. Feel the textures of leaves, of pets' fur. Appreciate small speak with buddies.

An expansive lifestyles overflows with modest yet profound joys that fee not anything. Fulfillment is dwelling not in frantic chasing, however in awed receiving of what already surrounds you.

Pursue Your Purpose Passionately

Your unique items lengthy to be expressed. Discover your non-public passions, then pursue them with relentless devotion.

Let your life become centered spherical something makes you lose track of time - artwork, volunteering, entrepreneurship, writing. Follow callings till they come to be the holy paintings only you can do.

Your cause is not about fame or achievement. It is the journey itself - residing with ever-developing authenticity, braveness and coronary heart. Let this guide you.

Give and Receive Freely

Cultivate wholesome connections that encourage mutual increase. Give beneficial resource freely then graciously get maintain of it as properly.

Spend time with emotionally to be had, compassionate individuals who have interplay your spirit. Share your actual self and stories. Offer kindness with out searching ahead to a few issue in flow again, sincerely for its private sake.

In every giving and receiving, live anchored for your wholeness. Fulfilling relationships ultimately boom your non-public mild, in location of entire you.

Trust Your Inner Wisdom

Listen for your intuitive voice for steerage. It whispers underneath the floor, guiding you to growth and reason.

Tune out outside noise and distractions. In stillness, create space for internal recognize-the manner to emerge. Then have the courage to act upon it, regardless of the fact that others doubt you.

As you comply with your inner compass over the evaluations of others, self-trust deepens. You reclaim your authority to live through your non-public slight and reality.

Love Radiates Endlessly

When you nurture unconditional love inner, it cannot help however radiate outwards, touching all you meet. Others experience its warm temperature, respond in kind, and bypass it on.

You overflow with compassion for human flaws and struggles, which incorporates your non-public. You forgive resultseasily, embody brazenly, deliver generously from this countless internal deliver.

And have to each other's love bless your adventure within the destiny, it will supplement the wholeness you have got decided - now not entire you, however go along with the flow harmoniously alongside your personal perfect slight.

## Chapter 7: Psychology Of Holding On

Humans very own an awesome ability of remembrance of the beyond that lets in us to study from it and modify to our surroundings whereas the fine element about maintaining onto the past cannot be overpasses. But whilst memories of the beyond collect to some extent whereby they end up an impediment to development, someone can experience weighed down with the aid of the usage of the use of reminiscence, an revel in that negatively influences emotion and hinders in addition boom. We will delve into why we keep to live at the past and its impact on our lives

The Seductive Pull of Nostalgia

Remember that human beings typically withstand changes which arise because of inherent intellectual inclinations toward the past. This conduct is stimulated thru numerous subjects:

1.  Emotional Attachments: Emotionally, hundreds folks experience a extraordinary

deal of affinity in the course of a few humans, gadgets and epochs. Its reference to comfort and a experience of safety makes it tough to detach at the same time as letting skip.

2. Fear of Uncertainty: In layman's phrases, the unknown destiny is horrifying. However, keeping onto the past offers a faux feel of safety even as what actually exists is instability and unpredictability.

3. Regret and Guilt: At times, we discover our past sins and feelings resurrected to taunt us on topics we would have omitted. If those feelings were allowed to stay inner parents, we'd experience punished for ourselves for no longer challenge a few thing.

four. Identity and Self-Image: Our beyond lifestyles permits us to experience like ourselves. It method that they want to be allow pass.

While clinging immediately to the beyond may additionally need to offer a fleeting enjoy of solace, it regularly has a terrible impact on our emotional and mental health:

five. Stagnation: Softly spoken the past remains stubborn and viscous. It is a problem to us advancing on existence and eventually ends up terminating our quest for modern day reports.

6. Relationship Strain: It could make, as properly, our efforts prone in growing partnerships with someone. At present we have a tendency to recall others and react to others because of our now not solved troubles.

7. Reduced Resilience: The more we cannot adapt, the much less resilient we turn out to be. The beyond can be such an obstacle because of that, hindering the capability to face existence's everlasting adjustments.

THE GUILT TRAP

Guilt is a complicated and ingrained emotion that frequently plays the feature of a ethical compass to guide our conduct along the right course in phrases of our social and moral duties. However, this form of repentance has a totally poor dimension which psychiatrists generally define as ' the guilt entice"

How to Avoid the Guilt Trap

Being responsible manner ordinary and acute emotions of sorrow approximately certain deeds or situations, however once in a while the guilt is groundless. It can take many one in each of a type paperwork and be inspired with the useful resource of every internal and outdoor factors:

1. Unrealistic Expectations: The Guilt entice arises whilst someone locations up with undue pressure on themselves. Though now not viable to gather, if the same antique is not met, one may moreover experience guilt and self-blame.

2. Perfectionism: The perfectionists are also liable to stumble into the guilt entice. The males and females are usually tough in their

self-complaint for any imaginary defects they will note about themselves.

three. Over-Responsibility: Guilt is regularly experienced while matters fail to schooling consultation according to plot or whilst incredible humans are adversely affected; due to the fact the man or woman taking on greater than their sincere percent of duty for someone else's amusement and welfare.

People-beautiful: When a person is willing toward safeguarding his/her likes, it makes her or him enjoy responsible if he / she prioritizes wonderful humans's goals over one's likes.

The Guilt Trap's Outward Signs

The guilt entice can take many precise forms and characteristic an effect on every highbrow and bodily fitness:

1. Rumination: Ruminators get trapped in their personal guilt because they will be generally preoccupied with mind of repeated

mistakes dedicated in previous encounters or sports sports.

2. Physical Breakdown: Physically, guilt may also result in a few signs and signs and signs collectively with complications, muscle tension, belly upsets or sleep disturbances.

Self-Punishment: Some humans practice self-punishment along with self-complaint, isolation or sabotage due to their belief of getting carried out something incorrect.

Decision-Making Impairment: The extra guilt can also prevent specific enough preference-making. Anxiety approximately hurting every self or others can also accentuate choice-making difficulties.

Beyond Good and Evil, The Guilt Trap.

The first step in escaping the guilt entice is cultivating an energetic recognition or self-recognition and having self-compassion. Here are some techniques to beneficial useful resource human beings in escaping its highbrow clutches:

1. Determine Unjustified Guilt: First, find out whilst guilt is over completed. Journaling may be a fantastic way to phrase certain regularities and triggers.

2. Self-Compassion Exercise: Show your self the equal compassionate mindset you may display for your closest friend. Understand that human beings have defects, Make errors.

3. Challenge Self-Talk: Aware your self of any crucial thoughts which you have and start to venture and redraft them absolutely. This can be carried out by way of changing those biases with greater rationalized and balanced perspectives.

4. Create clean limits in friendships, learn how to specific your desires and goals. Importantly, searching after oneself does no longer suggest one is being egotistical.

HOW GUILT KEEPS US STUCK

Guilts are very complex emotions that could paralyze us at severa tiers. It hinders us and forestalls us from shifting ahead in existence.

It destroys future and ambition if no longer well managed. Here are a number of the strategies in which guilt can prevent us from transferring in advance in life:

1. Ruminating on Past Mistakes: There is constantly a tendency for guilt to make us flow into lower back mentally in time and preserve repeating particular activities related to the errors made through us. It can be incessant, because of this that it maintains taking on our mind so we can not deal with the triumphing or consider the destiny.

2. Negative Self-Image: The presence of guilt can lower our self-understand and self-esteem. It is guilt that makes us expect there can be some aspect incorrect with us that forestalls us from being happy and succeeding in life. Such terrible photographs of ourselves restrict our development toward goals and goals.

three. Avoidance and Inaction: There are certain situations, humans or opportunities we are capable of keep away from when they remind us of our past disasters and they leave us feeling responsible. It also can additionally avoid publicity to novelty, thereby retarding self-improvement.

4. Relationship Strain: Feeling accountable makes it tough for us to interact with other people. There may be instances when we push away those who love us due to the fact we assume they don't deserve our love or choose us. In addition, guilt effects in quarrels and discrepancies which are skilled even in relationships.

five. Self-Punishment: Some people ought to punish themselves via self unfavorable behaviors due to the wrong picks that they made in advance. These elements may want to lead them to take pleasure in self sabotage, like substance abuse, as they weaken their spirit.

4. Stagnation: Guilt also can bring about monotony and passive acquiescence. These people may furthermore see themselves as

no longer worth of improvement or happiness of their personal and expert lives.

five. Difficulty in Letting Go: Feeling Guilty Can Render One Unforgivable To Oneself Or Others. Grudge or hate is preserving it alive with negativity, thereby hindering restoration and forgiveness.

RECOGNIZING UNHEALTHY GUILT

Guilt is a powerful and complex emotion that serves as a natural part of the human experience. In healthy doses, guilt can guide our behavior, supporting us navigate the ethical landscape and make decisions. However, like many emotions, guilt can grow to be bad even as it is immoderate or irrational. Unhealthy guilt can be negative to our mental and emotional properly-being, predominant to feelings of self-blame, low self-esteem, or even tension or despair.

Unhealthy guilt, frequently referred to as immoderate or irrational guilt, is an emotion that is going beyond the inexpensive bounds of responsibility or morality. While healthy guilt can motivate us to correct our moves and make amends when we have certainly done a few factor incorrect, unstable guilt includes feeling guilty even when we are now not at fault or when our guilt an extended way exceeds the scenario's importance.

Bellows are some of the approaches dangerous guilt may be recognized;

1. Overthinking and Rumination: Individuals experiencing unhealthy guilt tend to obsessively live on past activities or selections, replaying them in their minds. They continuously question themselves, wondering if they ought to have done things in every other way, despite the fact that that they had very little manage over the outcome.

2. Perfectionism: Unhealthy guilt often accompanies perfectionism. Individuals may additionally moreover furthermore set unrealistically excessive requirements for themselves and feel responsible when the

inevitably fall short, even if their efforts were commendable.

three. Self-Blame: People struggling with terrible guilt have a tendency responsible themselves for everything that is going wrong, no matter their actual involvement or responsibility. They internalize blame even when outdoor factors were at the entire responsible for the outcome.

4. Fear of Disapproval: Those plagued with the useful resource of unhealthy guilt are often overly concerned about how others perceive them. They also can feel accountable about disappointing others or not assembly their expectations, even though these expectancies are unreasonable or unrealistic.

5. Difficulty Saying "No": Unhealthy guilt can lead to an loss of potential to set obstacles and say "no" to requests or needs, no matter the reality that doing so would possibly be of their incredible interest. This worry of disappointing others drives them to address greater than they're capable of cope with.

Recognizing and handling bad guilt is vital for our intellectual and emotional nicely being. While guilt is a herbal emotion, it can turn out to be damaging at the same time as it's far excessive or irrational. By information the reasons and spotting the symptoms and signs and symptoms and symptoms and signs and symptoms of lousy guilt, you may take steps to deal with it and domesticate a extra healthful enjoy of self and relationships.

## SHAME AND SELF-WORTH

Shame is a complex emotion evolved at the same time as we take delivery of as real with we've got fallen short of our non-public or society's expectancies. It often manifests as a feel of unworthiness, imperfection, or fundamental badness. Unlike guilt, which facilities on the conduct or motion, disgrace centers at the person's perceived price as a person. It can be sparked with the useful resource of way of a range of things, along with mistakes, complaint, rejection, or maybe unrealistic societal norms.

Shame is a robust and often painful emotion that can profoundly have an effect on one's sense of self-worth. Although it is a standard human revel in, the methods wherein it influences our lives range extensively from person to person. Understanding the relationship among disgrace and self-worth is crucial for one's essential properly being, highbrow fitness, and personal development.

Shame's Effect on Self-Worth

1. Negative Self-Recognition: Shame can skew our perception of ourselves, fundamental us to simply accept as actual with that we're basically incorrect or unworthy of affection and recognition. This bad self-image may purpose one to revel in an awful lot less valuable.

2. Self-complaint: People who revel in disgrace are regularly pretty self-essential. They may want to regularly criticize themselves for perceived flaws, which similarly damages their self-esteem.

3. Isolation: Feeling ashamed frequently motives people to retreat socially due to the truth they fear approximately being judged or rejected via others. Isolation ought to make humans sense more unworthy.

4. Perfectionism: Some people respond to disgrace through pursuing perfection an outstanding manner to save you enduring emotions of inadequacy in the future. But this quest for fantastic perfection may be draining and dangerous to 1's experience of nicely truly well worth.

Breaking The Shameful Chains

1. Self-Compassion: A sturdy treatment for disgrace is studying to be awesome and compassionate to oneself. Treat yourself with the equal compassion and forgiveness which you could provide to a pricey buddy who had wronged you.

2. Defeat Negative Beliefs: Realize that the ideals and mind originating from disgrace aren't intention facts. Challenge those faux

beliefs with the useful resource of searching out proof to the opportunity and converting the way you communicate to your self.

three. Seek Support: Shame regularly flourishes in solitude. Reach out to trusted friends, own family people, or a therapist who can offer a steady, accepting environment in order to precise and paintings thru your feelings.

four. Practice Vulnerability: When we percentage our memories with others, shame regularly loses its strength. Accept your vulnerability through being open approximately your struggles and fears with people you may depend upon for empathy and expertise.

five. Self-reputation and mindfulness: You can emerge as more aware of your emotions and mind through engaging in aware practices. This attention may be a beneficial tool for identifying and managing shame when it manifests.

6. Set low-cost expectations: Set unrealistic requirements that could have contributed in your shame to project. Recognize that perfection is unachievable and that it's far best to make errors and study from them.

7. Professional Assistance: In a few situations, disgrace may be deeply ingrained and necessitate the supervision of a intellectual fitness professional. Therapy can provide beneficial capabilities and techniques for addressing disgrace and reestablishing one's experience of worth.

## THE DESTRUCTIVE NATURE OF SHAME

It changed into already stated above that disgrace is a completely unfavorable feeling that could cause excessive results for someone's intellectual and emotional nicely-being. Unlike guilt which concerns regrets for precise acts, disgrace is an assault at one's center identification. Usually this is related to mind that a person is terrible, now not worthy, and essentially faulty. Now we are capable of look at how the feeling of embarrassment can harm someone's inner-self, at the side of its underlying motives, results and strategies for overcoming it.

What Causes Shame?

It can be due to various factors like adolescence traumas, pressures imposed with the aid of the use of using society or perhaps deficiencies inside one's non-public lifestyles. Here are some usual motives of shame:

1. Childhood Experiences: Negative or judgemental parenting may additionally moreover sow shame in a person's life, further to any disturbing evaluations whilst a child. With such critiques, there is a threat of sporting them into maturity with the resource of these children.

2. Social and cultural factors: Frequently, society establishes no longer feasible dreams for one's achievement, splendor, behavior. People may experience disgrace for now not appearing nicely as it is perceived that society

has immoderate expectations approximately them.

three. Personal Mistakes and Failures: Shame over beyond mistakes, whether or now not or no longer it is a minor oversight or critical life mistake. These evaluations need to make a person begin wondering his or her self confidence as one loses self guarantee in themselves.

Destructive Effects of Shame.

1. Low Self-Esteem: Shame destroys arrogance which in the long run outcomes in an person seeing themselves very lowly. Shamed human beings regularly experience as even though they're faulty, now not worth of love and not able to be successful.

2. Isolation and Loneliness: The folks that enjoy ashamed would probably exclude themselves traumatic about what exclusive count on. This isolation might also additionally moreover get worse a paralyzing

cycle of disgrace and intensify emotions of "not-being-correct-enough".

three. Addiction, despair, and anxiety are a number of the numerous highbrow issues which may be cautiously tied with shame. These illnesses can be brought about thru the improvement of disgrace-related poor self communicate and extended frequency of self-grievance.

4. It may be harder to shape healthy relationships because of shame. People who've been deeply humiliated will be predisposed to have hassle speaking, confiding in others, or expressing their emotions, which over time erodes their relationship with buddies and family.

Leaving Shame Behind

1. Self-Compassion: Developing self-compassion is one of the most vital tiers in conquering shame. Treat your self as a chum who is experiencing comparable times, be

kind and gentle together along with your coronary coronary heart.

2. Challenge Your Negative mind: Admit the mind which can be available in conjunction in conjunction with your embarrassment are faux. There are special methods of dispelling the ones notions with the useful resource of looking at counter arguments and converting the way you deal with your self.

3. Vulnerability and Connection: To wreck this chain, one ought to be open to talking approximately their studies and emotions and percentage them with reliable people. This form of isolation can be eased through way of manner of forging hyperlinks which may be apparent and real from the begin.

four. Self-Awareness and Mindfulness: These techniques will help you word, but no longer interpret or label your feelings and mind. Shame need to emerge in this awareness which can be a powerful weapon of spotting it and dealing with it up.

## REBUILDING SELF WORTH

Self nicely worth paperwork the idea of a healthful and happy lifestyles. It is the bedrock of our self-worth in which the manner that we see our skills, value and region on this global takes root. One's very very personal perception in a unmarried's fee as an character. However, now and again, there may be complications of life; defeats, unfair experience, self-evaluation with others, perfectionism, unsightly memories, traumatization, and other varieties of abuse.

How Important Self-Worth Is

It is damage away outside factors including accomplishments, look or what others anticipate. People with a excellent feeling of self-worth can:

1. Set and Pursue objectives: When we believe in our skills, we will be predisposed to be outstanding and decided to reap any purpose or goal that seems out of gather.

3 Establish Healthy Boundaries: By having high esteem about ourselves we're capable of layout as properly preserve sound barriers in our relationships, thereby ceasing reputation of disrespect/abuse.

four Handling adversity frequently consists of resilience and self confidence. Those who enjoy virtually worth effortlessly manage strain and disasters.

REBUILDING SELF-WORTH: PRACTICAL STEPS

1 Practice Self-Care: When people apprehend themselves as treasured, it method that they have the proper to be glad and properly. Thus, they will deal with their our our our bodies and thoughts. Practice self-compassion! Love yourself as you like your buddy. Embrace your shortcomings and be mild approximately your self, due to the fact you had a feature in what occurred.

2. Challenge Your Negative Beliefs: Unmasking your self-condemning questioning patterns. Check for their validity; find out why

they will be wrong. Use high-quality alternatives and clever thinking with this stuff.

3. Establish Small, Achievable Goals: Set small dreams that could without problems be completed to regain your self assurance and experience successful another time. Regardless of their period, honor all your accomplishments.

four. Seek Support: Talk to cherished ones, close to buddies, or a therapist this is willing to provide you emotional guide further to steerage at the equal time as strolling in the direction of redeeming your self-admire. It is also restoration to percent your demanding situations with those you're very near along with buddies and/or family.

5. Self-Awareness and Mindfulness: Learn to be aware about your mind and revel in them, however with out categorization the usage of mindfulness strategies. Self interest lets in one to study such styles and alter them even as essential.

6. Put reputation on yourself care wherein it topics most. Focus on self-care. It may involve participating into pleasure sports activities activities like undertaking a recreation or hobby this is exciting, balanced diets and proper relaxation.

PART 2

THE HEALING PROCESS

The capability to forsake is an essential flair which could result in noteworthy mending within the super texture of lifestyles. The getting higher approach is a transformative excursion that smooths out a way for improvement, strength, and self-revelation, whether or not or no longer you're coping with the outcomes of a separation, the passing of a chum or family member, a essential life flow into, or clearly endeavoring to launch unpleasant feelings. Let us take a look at the profound mending way and the way it buddies with the education of leaving behind.

Knowing How To Heal

It requires staying power, problem and regard for oneself to journey alongside the complex, various path of recovery. This route is not truthful; alternatively, there are various levels and tiers which might be all essential to the recuperation method. Herein lies a breakdown of usually what is worried in recovery:

1. Acknowledgement: The preliminary bypass towards healing is admitting that there is a few component looking to be addressed. Acknowledging distress, trauma, or emotional turmoil may be crucial to advantage this. It is important to take heed to one's feelings and take transport of them as a valid part of their adventure.

2. Grieving and mourning: Emotions constitute a critical problem inside the healing approach. Death and heartache in truth result

in responses of melancholy, pain, anger, and on occasion even upward thrust up. Instead of criticizing yourself, it's far important to offer yourself the freedom to lament and grieve.

3. Releasing: Releasing is the cornerstone of recuperation. It necessitates letting skip of ties to the long past days, the possible future, and the ugly emotions which keep you limited. Cultivating the functionality to allow pass can be very beneficial in this example.

4. Self-compassion is crucial for mending. Granting oneself pardon and admittance of 1's deficits are also factors of self-compassion. Nothing that has taken region to you has been your negligence.

True restoration regularly ensues from embracing the things that can't be changed and centering on what can be controlled. Acknowledging is not synonymous with endorsement; as an alternative, it is the belief that sure things are past the reap of one's have an effect on. Recovery is a opportunity for self-improvement. It can also bring about extended electricity, compassion, and a more potent attention of oneself and those around them.

PRACTICAL STEPS TO SELF FORGIVENESS

You once in a while say or do property you later regret. If this has happened these days, you may be finding it tough to forgive your self, mainly in case your actions introduced on someone you care about pain.

I had been given into an altercation with a pal a few months ago. It happened fast and , as most misunderstandings do. I no longer frequently had time to method what changed into taking place.

I lightly attempted to refuse my friend's invitation to sign up for him in a commercial enterprise organisation. After some back and forth, I misplaced persistence with him and he commenced out to come out more as a pushy salesman than a chum.

Then he said some issue that I took to be a private jab. I exploded out of anger right away. I first of all believed that my response changed into justified, however after a few attention, I identified that I had misconstrued his comments and made a snap choice.

I persevered to feel accountable approximately my error even after a look at-up verbal exchange in which I apologized in entire. I turn out to be concerned that our bond should trade over time.

That incident in my existence were given me considering how we commonly tend to consciousness on our private shortcomings. They have the capability to determine who we are going ahead and preserve us mired within the beyond.

I've provide you with the subsequent seven steps for forgiving yourself based completely mostly on my very personal reflected photo and enjoy:

1. Describe Your Actions: To be capable of forgive oneself, you need to recognize what passed off. Start via way of jotting down the specifics of what passed off and what you probable did to make a contribution to the predicament.

Avoid setting any blame on one in every of a kind human beings or outdoor factors and hold your interest handiest on your self. When acting this hobby, you will likely feel exceptionally willing. Instead of denying this vulnerability, embrace it with love.

In my non-public case, I targeted on my buddy's out of character violent behavior to manual my movements. I may want to peer extra sincerely that I had judged his statements too fast as quickly as I became inclined to consciousness by myself moves.

2. Make An Apology: Begging for forgiveness is tough. You are acknowledging you made a mistake and are sorry for it in case you are inclined to speak to a person you have got harm.

Avoid using terms like "I'm sorry if" or "I'm sorry but" to downplay your duties. I turn out to be aware that I had to specific my remorse to my friend and take transport of complete duty for what I had finished. I truly stated my mistake and begged for pardon.

three. Forgive yourself if damaging mind floor. Even after receiving forgiveness, we occasionally have problem forgiving ourselves.

I felt accountable and had regretful thoughts approximately what I had carried out even after my friend and I had labored matters out. I eventually understood that forgiving oneself is a extended technique in area of a one-time act. I may additionally want to take a deep breath in and permit all the negativity out whenever I had thoughts of self-loathing. When unfavorable thoughts start to creep in, you may do a little element comparable for your self.

4. Be appreciative of your mistakes: To be satisfied about our errors, in particular the

painful and humiliating ones, may also moreover appear abnormal. But bear in mind a time whilst you made a mistake or did some issue you later regretted. How has the come across altered you? Did it come up with greater facts, energy, or prudence?

I came to apprehend the perils of being quick with humans and jumping to conclusions. I now make the effort to allow myself some time and area when I am unhappy so that I can contemplate rather than react. I'm thankful for the threat to reinforce in those techniques.

You also may be happy to your screw ups if you can learn how to view them in this way— as possibilities to enhance.

5. Love yourself absolutely in each manner: A quote from Joseph Campbell goes, "The privilege of an entire lifestyles is being who you are." Be who you're and now not who you had been in the past. In spite of, or probable even because of, your past errors,

be glad with who you've got were given turn out to be.

My buddy has visible me for who I am now due to my very own shortcomings, that allows you to ultimately make our connections stronger in the future. Love your self for who you are, mistakes and all, and you can excellent turn out to be more potent as a cease result.

6. You Are Deserving of Pardon: These moves aren't usually smooth to carry thru, especially while we've clearly screwed up. However, we might also additionally pass on from our mistakes, observe from them, and forgive ourselves.

You are deserving of your very own affection and pardon. Have entire and utter religion in it.

Even on the times on the same time as you will choose now not to, make a willpower to the usage of the ones techniques each day.

Make a selection to forgive yourself. Make a choice to permit bypass of the beyond. Decide to stay in the now. And keep an fine and hopeful outlook at the future.

THE KEY TO LETTING GO

Each people has prolonged beyond via durations of each bodily and emotional discomfort. Being annoyed due to the ache may be very regular. The difference is that a few human beings hold directly to those painful reminiscences longer than others, making it extra difficult for them to move on with their life. It's everyday to emerge as caught and replay your enjoy, however you need to in the end learn how to placed the beyond and future out of your mind and provide attention to the proper proper here and now. It's time to grasp the artwork of letting pass. The keys to letting circulate are highlighted beneath:

1. Express Your Pain Verbally: Don't suppress your feelings if you're experiencing pain or infection. Feeling your awful emotions the

identical manner you revel in your exquisite ones is k. It's ordinary for people to experience disappointment and grief now and again, but it is awful to permit those emotions rule your lifestyles and supply upward push to in addition ones.

Unleash your emotions and use any method vital to supply the subjects that ache you. Find your voice and make your mind diagnosed. Scream, cry, write your thoughts down, shout them out loud despite the fact that no character is listening—do a little aspect it takes to get the misery out of your body. This will can help you take shipping of the event and located it in the beyond with the useful useful resource of allowing you to realise the way you without a doubt enjoy approximately it and why it impacts you.

2. Decide To Let Go Of Something: To completely do away with the ones terrible emotions on the identical time as you feel like they will be taking over too much room on your coronary heart and head, you must first

decide that you want to change. Learning to allow skip requires a planned self-control and preference. Make a willpower to your desire as well as to your self. Try to save you thinking about the past critiques after that. Even even though it is difficult on the begin, you could finally comprehend how some distance you have got are available on account that making this option and what shape of you have advanced.

Here, strength of will is essential. Distract your mind and preserve in thoughts your dedication each time you revel in like residing at the specifics of a problem or turning into irritated approximately the matters that harmed you all all over again. Accept a latest, greater healthful manner of residing and awareness on drawing training from those horrifying studies.

three. Accept Reality As It Is: It takes vicinity frequently that you discover yourself replaying frightening occasions and going over each nuance that makes you harm. You won't be able to stay a entire lifestyles if you want that these moments had been certainly one of a kind. Unfortunately, no longer something may be finished to trade what has already befell; now not whatever may be completed to trade the past. Accept reality and prevent seeking to recreate an event that can not be changed.

Going lower back to a story that generally results in distress is vain. This will truely cause you to relive that suffering, that may cause similarly self-harm. The excellent factor you may do is renowned the problem and be organized for the destiny in vicinity of persevering with to inform your self the same tale. Let's say you ever discover your self in a similar scenario. You'll recognize the manner to deal with conditions better so that you do no longer enjoy pain another time.

4. Quit Blaming Other People: The maximum not unusual reaction to painful situations is to region the blame on others. You may additionally moreover keep to accept as

actual with that someone has wronged you, and the possibility character also can moreover have the equal opinion of you. Even blaming your self, absolving your self of responsibility, and blaming a person else who can also or might not be at fault may additionally sense outstanding.

It's suitable to name for an apology in those times, pressure a person to very private as lots as their movements, or revel in as despite the fact that the culprit should undergo similarly to you. The truth is that on the equal time as you characteristic your struggling on someone else, you're absolutely granting them the ability to control your emotions. This genuinely prevents you from exciting.

Like I said formerly, you need to widely recognized that subjects are as they're and that putting blame on others will now not modify what happened. Therefore, save you pointing the finger at others, very own up for your thing inside the trouble, and flow into on.

five. Find Support From Those Who Make You Happy: Spend time with humans that really care approximately you and quality want the super for you. Keep in thoughts that those mother and father, whether or not or no longer or not they're your own family or friends, are commonly there for you.

Find ethical resource in the those who make you glad; talk with them and specific your feelings. Get every unpleasant emotion out of your device at the equal time as being conscious that you are in a honest setting. Listen to them out as they provide you with an interloper's mind-set which will permit you to view the problem from a smooth attitude. Even if their critiques differ out of your private, take into account them surely and with an open mind.

The exceptional difficulty you could do in case you find out your self living with the ones that don't beautify your life is to region a long way amongst yourself and them. Creating this distance amongst you and needless human beings can now and again be a extraordinary step in the direction of letting pass.

6. Pay Attention To What Makes You Happy Right Now: I understand that getting to know to allow skip of things may be difficult, but to make the approach extra bearable, you have to try to stay in the 2d and make the maximum of it. Continue your day with high-quality thoughts and satisfying sports. When the soreness starts offevolved to weigh down you, take a harm by means of doing some element that makes you happy proper now.

Making room for emblem spanking new reviews way putting the beyond behind you and concentrating on the prevailing. Your mind might be freed of all the awful feelings as a end end result, allowing you to create clean thoughts to help you growth. Soon after letting go, you could see that it have grow to be the extraordinary selection you can have made due to the reality that you may be more open to pride and happiness for your lifestyles.

Give up a cherished one which makes it difficult as a way to enjoy the pleasure you desire. Give up a method that motives you pain. And allow pass of unsightly reminiscences.

HOW TO MAKE AMENDS, APOLOGIES AND RESTITUTION

There are few, only a few, in an effort to very very very own themselves in a mistake.

However, no matter the fact that the repercussions of this is probably severe, few human beings are aware about the manner to catch up on a mistake. If you do not express regret for awful conduct, it could badly damage each your popularity and your relationships. We'll take a look at a manner to acquire duty for a mistake and the manner to take some time to make matters proper.

Making amends and apologizing are various matters. Simply pronouncing "I'm sorry" to a person you have got irritated is considered an apology. Making apologies includes taking steps to accurate the wrong you have got completed and reestablish concord with the opportunity person.

Imagine, for instance, if you said some aspect carelessly that made a coworker's self notion collapse. You may additionally want to make apologies thru using assigning that man a venture as a way to restore his self belief after virtually apologizing.

Admitting which you've made a mistake may be very uncomfortable. Many human beings discover it tough to really take transport of that they have got made a mistake due to the truth it's far entering into competition to the grain of the ego. However, making apologies has plenty of advantages.

Consider the individual you've got were given wronged first. You offer them a risk to forgive you whilst you make an apology and make restitution.

When people hold grudges and agree with they were wronged, the ones mind purpose unsightly emotions, extended blood pressure, and physical stress. However, human beings experience more on pinnacle of factors of the state of affairs and are a amazing deal less forced even as they will be able to forgive wrongs.

Making Apologies Is Also Worthwhile For Personal Reasons.

You can regain your self-recognize via accepting responsibility for your remarks or movements. When you admit your mistakes, you could permit flow of pervasive feelings of shame and the conviction which you're acting improperly through using "ducking the hassle."

Additionally, while you in reality and brazenly express regret, you may truely enhance a connection. You can display that you care approximately the alternative character and which you are sincerely sorry for what came about via being humble sufficient to make matters proper. Both of you could enjoy higher if the other individual can forgive you.

Making apologies can even help you boom your integrity, a rare and acceptable quality, in addition in your personal reputation. This is critical in a professional putting. Making an attempt to make subjects proper demonstrates humility and empathy and might considerably increase your consider internal your business company.

Making amends also can gift opportunities for analyzing. By considering what went incorrect and what needs to be achieved in any other manner inside the future, you are concentrating on arising with a higher solution the following time.

Let's recall the exceptional way to start making subjects right.

Step 1: Recognize Your Role In The Situation

After committing a mistake, deliver your self a while to accumulate your mind and maintain in mind what went wrong, but don't wait too prolonged to begin making amends. This prevents resentment and fury from developing.

Recognize your component in the situation to start. When they have achieved a few factor wrong, people on occasion try and cowl in the back of emotions of guilt, hostility, or defensiveness. They may moreover additionally even attempt to persuade themselves that that they had no preference however to act in the manner they did. However, it's far probable that your "gut instinct" will tell you that you have committed a incorrect, especially if it has caused damage to every other individual.

Then, reflect onconsideration on things from the factor of view of the alternative birthday party. What effect did your errors have on his existence? Did you disappoint the man or woman? Did you make him sense uncomfortable or irritated? You can learn how to experience empathy for specific people via noting how your moves hurt the opportunity individual or speaking approximately it with a pal.

It's moreover a important first step for the reason that without expertise your feature inside the incident, you could not be capable of make amends and properly mend fences with the opportunity party.

Step 2: Plan Your Approach

Determine what you can do to restore the harm. This consists of reestablishing self assurance and apologizing in your errors.

It's essential which you generate some proper ideas. Remember to talk to the opportunity character that you are aware of your errors and its results. Token movements will satisfactory start to mend the strained dating; they may not simply treatment the hassle.

Your reaction need to bring about a revel in of equilibrium and useful useful resource in the extraordinary man or woman's improvement or healing. If you are dubious of whether or not or not your response is suitable, communicate the situation with a dependable friend, member of the family, mentor, or coworker.

Avoid overcompensating at the equal time as feeling accountable. The hazard with this is that you could come out as insincere, that may exacerbate an already difficult situation. In an try to restore the relationship, you can additionally find out yourself taking over an excessive amount of and disappointing others inside the method.

If you are having problem figuring out whether or not or now not your endorsed direction of motion is excessive, talk your thoughts with a pal or coworker.

Consider using function-playing techniques to workout the talk after you have were given developed your approach. You'll be capable of expect the opportunity person's feelings and reply to them greater correctly in case you prepare your apologies.

Step 3: Communicate Your Intentions

You have to supply numerous key factors on your announcement of choice to make amends.

First, apologize for your errors and receive duty for what occurred. For instance: "I'm truely sorry that I did now not observe via on my promise that will help you complete your venture on Friday."

After that, supply an reason for the way your conduct impacted the opportunity character and particular your appreciation for his or her emotions. Hold yourself accountable and avoid playing the "blame endeavor." Demonstrate your know-how of the mistake of your strategies.

Example: "After promising to help, it have become egocentric of me now not to. I can recognize that you is probably experiencing the same emotions proper now. In this condition, I should have been upset and sour. You needed to work substantially tougher than you may have if I'd been there due to my absence. Additionally, yourself guarantee in me has decreased due to my absence.

Tell them how vital you discover their relationship to be. For instance: "Your don't forget is really important to me, and I want to set topics right."

Make up for it. Example: "I apprehend which you requested my help due to the know-how I must have furnished. I want to make amends for it. Allow me to help you this week on every night time till the undertaking is finished and you could post the findings.

Step four: Learn From Your Mistakes

Make sure you spot the honestly really worth of what occurred after you have expressed remorse and made restitution. Mistakes will will let you enhance in case you take the time to examine from what took place. They are useful education gear.

Ask yourself without a doubt why you reacted the way you did after considering the times that brought up to date. Do you have got a difficult time controlling your feelings? Did you estimate a task's of entirety time incorrectly? Or is a few factor about your process making you traumatic?

What should you do to save you this from happening once more?

## EXTRACTING WISDOM FROM ERRORS: A JOURNEY OF GROWTH

Mistakes are woven into the fabric of life itself, that is made from a thread. Nobody has lived with out making errors at some point of their lives. However, such occurrences must not be written off as a simple mistake due to the reality they could serve as a gold mine for perception and personal improvement. Being capable of increase and analyze from errors is a key detail of what it way to be human. This e-book explores how learning from our failures can assist us make profound discoveries and beautify our development

1. The First Essential Step Is Self-Reflection: The basis for gaining knowledge of from

mistakes is self-reflected photograph. We study our options, actions, and outcomes as a part of the system. We are taught to address our errors head-on with self-reflected photo, asking what and the way every mistake changed into made. This is a crucial first step that permits us to recognize the muse motives of the error.

2. Acceptance: Accepting Your Imperfections: Acceptance is the essential aspect to unlocking the analyzing hidden in beyond errors. Most of the time, people find out it tough to accept their mistakes because of the truth they trust it makes them appear unlikable. However, such actual development can fine begin via manner of acknowledging mankind. The fact that we are all human and percent this experience in desire to the truth that we make mistakes is what makes us willing. Embracing Our Imperfections Means Accepting Past Mistakes.

three. Identifying and Analyzing Patterns: Errors do no longer appear in a vacuum.

These encounters monitor numerous normal human behaviors associated with our choices. This allows us apprehend the underlying issues that reason our mistakes. For example, if we frequently come upon situations with the equal very last results, it may be critical to alter our intellectual techniques, standards for making choices, or sporting activities.

4. Solving Issues: A Talent Forged in Mistake.

It's beneficial to draw instructions from the beyond whilst seeking to solve a hassle. There should be a awesome repair for each errors. In the future, we may be able to deal with a state of affairs like this one better. Among unique system, hassle-solving facilitates us recognize a way to address troubles in our lives.

five. Personal Development: A Personal Reformation Journey for Life-Long Self Reform: We get further statistics about the world and ourselves with each mistake we make. These sorts of stories help us increase emotionally and spiritually. Life development, like each initiation adventure, consists of in advance mistakes that characteristic stepping stones for the future.

## 6. Resilience: The Ability to Recover from Failure

Making mistakes emotionally drains you. Making up for our faults well-knownshows who we're. When we've got a take a look at from our beyond errors, we grow to be stronger. Errors can't define our lifestyles or assist us in firmly and bravely overcoming next limitations.

## 7. Knowledge Exchange: A Generous Deed

Through sharing their knowledge and notion with others, they had been capable of have a look at from their mistakes and persuade others that they need to not excursion down the same path. Our information may also be helpful to human beings going via similar conditions. Because they foster a revel in of belonging that encourages assist a few of the ones professions, sharing consequently is going beyond sincerely giving and as an alternative contributes to a shared human wealth.

PART three

THE POWER OF THE PRESENT MOMENT

We can with out troubles discover ourselves looking continuously forward into the destiny and backward into the past as we stay in our all of sudden converting global. Our present slip thru our palms as we continuously play with severa duties, troubles, and sorrows. The capability of the prevailing second for transformation is what we are able to use to live a satisfied, calm, and happy existence.

1. The Transient Character of Time: Time, however, feels slippery and fleeting, nearly like a mirage. As a 2nd moves in advance, it could in no manner be retrieved because it becomes beyond. It is aware that element is fleeting, and because of this it underscores the nice gift we absolutely have is that this very second. Recollections are all that the

beyond consists of; the future being an unknown quantity. By staying in 'the now' we will have complete appreciation for the richness of life unfolding within the the front people.

2. The Key Is Mindfulness: The Secret of Presence: Mindfulness technique being sincerely in the gift 2d in absence of any distractions or intellectual judgments. This is an ability to live existence in the right here-and-now, appreciating extra every enjoy absolutely aware. Mindfulness consists of interest of 1's thoughts, feelings, somatosensory stories, and the surrounding surroundings. Mindfulness permits us to launch the strength inherent within the here-and-now and really live.

three. Stress control: With current-day existence's duties, in recent times one is regularly exposed to stress and problems. Worry about the past or brooding over it can damage our intellectual and emotional well being. However, the modern time is an break out from chaos – the chaos of notions and issues for the subsequent time. When we live present, stress disappears and lets in us to revel in cushty and serene.

four. Improved Relations: Similarly, the contemporary 2nd additionally influences our relationships with one-of-a-kind humans. When we're absolutely present, we happen a real interest or empathy in our conversations and interactions. Active listening, provision of assist, and being attentive to our instant organizations fosters a deep inter connection. Being present proper right right here is an existence there can be a reality.

five. Greater Recognition: By being in the now, we are able to see the marvel and the beauty of lifestyles which often bypass unnoticed. From the complex kinds of a snowflake to the warm temperature of the sun's rays upon our pores and skin, there can be an abundance of little subjects we are able to enjoy every day in this worldwide. This lets in us to pride in such moments of beauty and revel in lifestyles's small pleasures.

6. Self-Reflection And Development: Personal improvement relies upon on self-popularity. By staying within the gift we may be aware of our thoughts, feelings and conduct. Being acutely aware of the ones objects can help us to make higher choices and react honestly to demanding situations existence gives to us. The gift 2d is so robust that we come to be aware about our potential to conform.

7. Taking Advantage of Chances: Always open are possibilities in existence. By final truly grounded in the present 2d, it safeguards us in opposition to lacking out on life's possibilities, which include going for our passions, building relationships, and exploring profession possibilities. Living in the gift permits us to maximize possibilities that come inside the route folks.

Therefore, the power of the prevailing can trade or boom our lives in hundreds of methods. CULTIVATING MINDFULNESS AND

AWARENESS IN THE PRESENT MOMENT CAN LESSEN STRESS AND GAIN DEEPER APPRECIATION FOR THE BEAUTY OF LIFE. By using it we are capable of develop and modify whilst exploiting opportunities to be had at gift moments. Thus, inhale and breathe, be located in in that you are, as this is in which we find out the genuine which means of lifestyles.

LETTING GO THROUGH MINDFULNESS

Mindful letting bypass could be very profound in relinquishing clingy feelings, horrible feelings and undesired thoughts. Mindfulness non hobby is presence, a energy for people to create an recognition of non-movement permitting themselves to go away from demanding about the beyond or the destiny. Here's how mindfulness allows the approach of letting cross:

1. Awareness: To begin with, you need to be quite acutely aware of your thoughts, emotions, and physical sensations. Close announcement of your very very own inner

evaluations without judgment can will permit you to end up aware of the psyche-emotional styles which pull you decrease back into regression or challenge in advance.

2. Observing Without Judgment: With the mindfulness technique, one does meditation approximately the mind and feelings in order not to installation their ethical price. In terrific terms, it implies that you categorize no notion as being suitable or terrible and none of things approximately you as such trouble. They seem proper earlier than your eyes, however you do not act in any respect.

three. Present-Centered Focus: At its middle, being aware entails anchoring oneself actually in the gift which will shift one's interest inside the route in their very very own emotions at some level inside the second. You can do that with the resource of focusing on your breathing or the physical feelings and surroundings round your body.

four. Non-Attachment: Mindfulness embraces non-attachment in mind and feelings. They aren't ones which you maintain to or resist, like clouds fading from the blue sky. It frees one from the beyond traumas consequently disengaging from rumination.

five. Acceptance: Put surely, being conscious way embracing with an open coronary heart what's currently transpiring. It's about acknowledging and embracing each the fantastic and nasty, because it were. Embracing the triumphing 2d completely allows releasing resistance and starting up to letting glide.

6. Dealing With Stress And Anxiety: However, for instance, it is applicable in mindfulness practice along with meditation and deep breath sporting activities which is probably used to launch strain. You can defeat such fears with the aid of the usage of certainly being inside the presence of your enemies or fears-you thereby prevent them taking manage of your emotions/thoughts with the useful resource of depriving them area.

7. Self-Compassion: It's the mindfulness that brings a chunk little little bit of self-compassion to give in. Self – compassion way extending the identical diploma of kindness, project and care to self that one has for a superb friend. By training self-compassion, one may also moreover release themselves from critiquing their errors and studies of regret.

8. Embracing Impermanence: According to mindfulness all subjects- concept, emotion and situations as well are transience . The recognition that existence itself is brief makes it possible for one to honestly be given adjustments and permit cross of an opinion as to what want to be happening continuously.

9. Reducing Rumination: Mindfulness is especially powerful to prevent ruminating as it technique refocusing on an item and therefore redirecting our interest from negative thoughts which consist of reliving beyond sports again and again again or imagining future concerns.

10 Cultivating Equanimity: It manner ultimate calm, quiet in instances of chance or trouble. It promotes equanimity, helping you allow pass of clinging into the beyond and traumatic too much about the destiny, lowering the emotional turbulence.

## EMOTIONAL RELEASE TECHNIQUES

Emotions play a very essential aspect in our lives however at instances they may be capable of turn out to be complicated and overpowering. Such lingering emotions like anger, unhappiness or strain may also additionally have an effect on our highbrow and physical fitness. In those cases, there may be a opportunity that the usage of ERT (Emotional Release Technique) will help to release emotional tension and create peace within the body, promoting happiness as a whole. An introduction to Emotional Release Therapy (ERT) and why it permit you to experience whole once more!

What are the Emotional Release Techniques? ERT releases repressed emotions and eases ache associated with feelings. It has been mounted and held that it's miles based mostly on a belief that emotions are bodily carried, and if one fails to clear up emotional subjects they may have bodily and intellectual fitness issues.

ERT is composed of things of numerous superb restoration modalities, collectively with somatic treatment, energy psychotherapy, and mindfulness; to facilitate the processing and exorcizing of repressed feelings from human beings's subconscious.

How Does ERT Function?

1. The Emotional Release Technique (ERT) calls for attention of one's emotions due to the fact the first step. It includes acknowledging the sensation, what introduced approximately it and the bodily sensations due to it.

2. Acceptance: Acceptance of emotion includes no interpretation or judgment via ERT. This consists of acknowledging emotions

with out labeling them as authentic or awful. Acceptance is one of the crucial ideas of mindfulness.

2. Body And Breath Awareness: ERT often entails mindfulness of your breath and bodily sensations. Recognition of breath and related physiological emotions will help you unwind or revel in secure.

three. Energetic Release (ERT): ERT considers the truth that emotions live internal an individual's lively gadget. Such strategies as acupressure or tapping come to be useful so you can set free the stagnant electricity of emotion. In ERT ,it is a common approach to poke at particular meridians on a factor to talk about what you revel in.

4. In ERT, expression is authorized in steady and moderated shape. This also can include writing or speaking about your emotions and revolutionary expression through artwork or track.

5. Self-Compassion: In this manner, ERT emphasizes that as we traverse our private emotional territory, compassion is critical; that we want to be moderate and sympathetic in the direction of ourselves.

The Advantages of ERT

1. Emotional Discharge: One of the maximum glaring advantages of ERT is the release of suppressed emotions thru discharge. Such an emotional catharsis will assist launch weight; make manner for brighter emotions.

2. Stress Reduction: ERT is an excellent anxiety reducer. Allow the emotional pressure to decrease, now you feel loose.

three. There Are Positive Effects To Processing And Eliminating Emotions On The Mind: These embody lessening of anxiety and depressive symptoms, higher emotional control and enhancement of normal emotional well-being.

four. Enhanced Physical Health: There is a normally famous perception, that the thoughts and the body are via some means associated with every exceptional. The intention of the test therefore is to diminish the terrible affects which come due to strain and feelings in our frame.

5. Better Relationships: Embracing imperfections approach that we permit ourselves to specific our emotions freely permitting others to connect on a deeper diploma than earlier than.

6. Personal Development: ERT enables individual formation with the resource of supporting people draw near and incorporating their emotions. This enhances self- evaluation and self- attention and contributes within the path of personal increase.

STRATEGY FOR MOVING FORWARD

Life route is complete of journey, with severa curves and swerves. One of the vital belongings, which allows us to navigate thru turmoil and get higher, is our ability to collect an go out direction, be it personal problems, career dilemmas, or worldwide struggles. This e-book goals at exploring techniques that could assist humans circulate earlier notwithstanding problem and uncertainty, allowing your functionality to confront existence's demanding situations with hobby and electricity.

1. Develop A Growth Mindset: Firstly, developing a subculture of growth orientation is the important step in the direction of improvement for improvement. In this manner, it embraces challenges as opportunities for increase and analyzing. In the case of a boom mentality, people are inclined to peer errors as an important a part of their ongoing boom in place of a failure that hinders them. Learn recognition about improvement, version and getting with the resource of using traumatic situations.

2. Define Specific Goals: This consists of placing smooth and sensible goals in advance. The purpose of that is to provide you a focus,

assisting you make a decision what it takes to fulfill your specific goals. Divide large goals into smaller obligations for which you could without problem lay down your improvement on roads. This approach gives concept and purpose in tough times.

3. Adopt Resilience: The functionality of people, businesses or society to get better in reaction to adversity or exchange. Without it, there may be no development. To come to be extra resilient, provide interest to surrounding your self with a wholesome assist tool; take care of yourself and keep a extremely good outlook. Resilience helps you to go through hard times in existence however live unbeaten.

4. Recognize Change: Life is changeful, and adopting exchange is crucial for one's destiny development. Instead, discover ways to receive modifications and skip in with them. Understand that even though they appear to be limitations on the start, modifications may

also result in some issue immoderate nice and create new reports and possibilities

five. Mindfulness And Living In The Present: Being conscious and present-centered permits moving in advance. This can recommend focusing most effective to your gift 2d, accepting it simply as it is, and letting pass of your concerns approximately your past and destiny. Through aware practices, you may discover ways to lessen pressure and anxiety that keep away from right selection making and provide you with an appreciation of yourself and what is going round.

6. Look for Connection and Support: It's now not lonely to move ahead is a word that translates into it. Talk with pals, circle of relatives, mentors, or manual organizations approximately it. Talking about issues and problems is shared emotionally with traumatic others, that could bring about enlightening conversations.

7. Draw Lessons From The Past: Learn from past encounters and errors a great way to get

understanding for the destiny. We have masses from our history. Who succeeded inside the beyond, who did not gain achievement? Reflecting on the past assist you to make higher alternatives, permitting no room for repeating antique errors.

eight. Look After Your Health: For earlier movement to be effective, one wants to be in fitness- physically and mentally. To keep preventing in the direction of setbacks one desires to do normal bodily bodily video games, maintain a balanced eating regimen, get sufficient sleep, and understand a way to control stress.

nine. Be Flexible: Flexible/adaptive method in a converting global will become as a substitute applicable for nowadays's art work surroundings. Be prepared to include new thoughts and to regulate your approach for that reason. Being capable of pivot and adapt to clearly new activities is an vital characteristic of achievement.

10. Imagine The Future You Want: Progress is fuelled by means of way of visualization. Picture your desired future as a supply of motivation.You may additionally additionally live advocated and focused to your dreams by way of visualizing the effects you want.

## Chapter 8: Understanding Worry And Over Thinking

What Worry and Over thinking really mean

Athorough attention of these intellectual foes is vital to reading the sector of letting move of strain and overthinking. What exactly are they? We use those phrases carelessly masses of the time, treating them like little annoyances that can be disregarded. But they will be lot more diffused and pernicious than they appear at the start.

Essentially, worry is the quit give up result of an innate protection mechanism in our brains. It is a survival approach that many generations of evolution have ingrained in our minds. Our predecessors used fear to weigh the risks, act speedy and in the long run assure their survival whilst faced with lifestyles-threatening conditions. Once useful in the wild, this instinctive response has now end up complex and multifaceted. Even if worry used to be nicely-intentioned, it has now grown immoderate and illogical, ensuing in anxiety and anxiety that frequently haven't any use.

Conversely, overthinking is the compulsive need to move over, reconsider and look at each choice and state of affairs. It resembles an obsessive investigator who in no manner shuts up. It can be beneficial reasonably, guiding our desire-making. But while overthinking receives out of hand, it is able to be crippling and hold us from moving ahead in any respect.

Overanalyzing and Anxiety: The Psychology behind It

We need to check the psychology of tension and overanalyzing so one can grow to be proficient inside the art of letting bypass.

These behaviors frequently have their origins in deeply rooted anxieties, worrying studies from the past, or social pressures. Disarming those behaviors' hold over us begins offevolved with an understanding in their psychological foundations.

Anxiety, that is carefully related to excessive fear, is due to an inflated notion of threats, an incapability to govern the future, or a dread of the unknown. Our mind, seeking to preserve us consistent, ad infinitum generate "what if" conditions that paralyze us with a in no way-finishing experience of dread. As the complexities of the human psyche are solved, fear is discovered out to be an wrong herbal reaction—a signal from our inner selves demanding our interest.

Overanalyzing additionally has robust psychological foundations. It usually has its roots in the worry of creating mistakes or being judged with the resource of others. This never-finishing exam is inspired thru an insatiable preference for readability and a desire to persuade clean of uncertainty. We are better succesful to interrupt loose from the grip that overthinking has on our existence the more we recognise the motives and triggers that bring about it.

Recognizing Patterns and Triggers

Being able to recognize the patterns and triggers that result in hassle and overthinking is critical to the technique of studying a way to allow pass. These triggers are as unique due to the truth the individuals who encounter them and there are numerous strategies in which styles can seem. By identifying them, we may also additionally moreover damage the pattern and take lower once more manage of our mind.

External triggers consist of factors like environmental pressures and hard lifestyles conditions. They may also moreover moreover come from interior, rooted in our ideas, convictions and previous encounters. Gaining the top hand in a combat in competition to an unseen foe is just like reading to pick out those triggers.

The recurrent notion patterns that maintain us demanding and overthinking are known as patterns. Rumination, perfectionism and catastrophic wondering are some examples of those. We may additionally begin the approach of breaking those inclinations and growing new, higher highbrow conduct by using recognizing them.

We will delve deeper into those factors of tension and overthinking in the imminent chapters, imparting you with the statistics and assets you want to defeat the ones enemies as quickly as and for all. By gaining knowledge, we set the degree for the alternate this is without a doubt throughout the corner and are led in the route of the danger of inner serenity and intellectual clarity.

THE TOLL ON HEALTH AND HAPPINESS

Physical and Emotional Consequences

The harsh truth of the negative results worry and overthinking have on our happiness and health want to be faced if one is to absolutely discover ways to permit skip of those awful conduct. The impact is not restrained to the mind; it ripples in the course of all factors of our lives, touching each area of our welfare.

First and number one, extended hassle and overthinking have critical terrible outcomes on one's fitness. Our our our our bodies go through considerably from the regular stress reaction, which releases a chain of hormones that bring about a huge form of illnesses. Unchecked anxiety will have a ways-reaching and probably deadly outcomes, starting from immune device damage to cardiovascular problems.

What's as essential are the emotional fallout. Our emotional materials are eroded via fear and overanalyzing, leaving us emotionally willing and empty. Our shallowness and famous emotional resilience are undermined on the identical time as we come to be stuck up in a never-completing loop of self-doubt and vital self-talk. Constant anxiety can cause impatience, withdrawal and misunderstandings with loved ones, which damages relationships. The emotional fallout from the ones occasions is a super load.

Case Studies and Empirical Illustrations

As a consultant within the location, I even have had the honour of supporting humans from some of backgrounds who're scuffling with anxiety and overthinking in their very very personal particular procedures. During my expert revel in, I honestly have in my view found the palpable and frequently disastrous results of these behaviors. Permit me to inform you the reminiscences of others who've confronted and overcome the ones disturbing situations.

Meet Sarah, a greater youthful professional whose anxiety of making errors and her incessant need for confirmation have held all over again her promising profession. Her tendency to overthink topics averted her from taking initiative, which introduced approximately misplaced opportunities and stagnant private development.

Or take John, a father who located it tough to revel in lifestyles on a every day basis for the reason that he turn out to be continuously concerned about his kid's destiny. He emerge as no longer able to allow skip of these troubles, which saved him from being really gift and interacting together together with his circle of relatives.

These are only a few instances of the innumerable lives which are trapped within the mazes of tension and overanalyzing. They offer as tangible evidence of the pressing need for change.

The Immediate Need for Adjustment

Nobody must should go through the terrible outcomes of worry and overthinking on their fitness and happiness. It is not feasible to magnify the want for change. If we keep going in the identical course, we are able to allow treasured moments bypass us via using, maintain a cycle of self-inflicted pain and decrease the standard of our lives.

The prospect of mental readability and internal calm isn't some a long way-off dream; as an opportunity, it is a completely actual capability that is inner attain. It is a promise of a life free of needless worry and one full of the small joys of everyday living. Change isn't first-rate a few problem we want; it is a smooth need for living a life this is large.

We will talk how to interrupt unfastened from the ones bonds and placed fitness and happiness again wherein they belong in your existence inside the pages that observe. Although the road requires bravery and backbone, the benefits are enormous. Accompany me on this adventure and collectively we're able to discover the way to a happier, greater gratifying existence.

## Chapter 9: The Roadmap To Inner Peace

Mindfulness and Present-Centered Awareness

The exercising of mindfulness and present-centered hobby is crucial to learning a manner to allow skip of pressure and overthinking. In your quest for internal peace, those practices can be your allies, retaining you grounded in the present now rather than turning into slowed down inside the rabbit holes of the past and destiny.

Developing a keen reputation of and reputation of the present day 2nd without passing judgment is the essence of mindfulness. It invitations you to satisfy your ideas, emotions and critiques head-on as they come up. By schooling mindfulness, you can reduce the have an impact on that your anxieties and thoughts have over your mind via studying to study them objectively. This exercising promotes intellectual readability and a deeper appreciation for the small pleasures in lifestyles.

Including mindfulness to your everyday activities may additionally have a profoundly quality impact. It helps you to get away the in no way-completing loop of overanalyzing through lightly bringing your interest once more to the proper right here and now. I will come up with useful bodily video games and recommendation on incorporating mindfulness into your existence as a topic remember quantity professional as a way to empower you to take manage of your thoughts and direct them closer to inner serenity.

Letting Go and Acceptance

Inner serenity is supported with the aid of the twin pillars of recognition and letting bypass. These techniques assist you apprehend your fears and issues and give you the self warranty to permit cross of them once they end up too much for you. They are about gaining knowledge of to stay with the thoughts that problem you and locating the braveness to allow them to move into the glide of lifestyles.

A deep hold close of what you could and can not manipulate is what is supposed through the usage of the usage of recognition, no longer resignation. You can unfastened yourself from the needless try and modify the unchangeable with the resource of embracing the truths of lifestyles. This technique helps you discover peace of thoughts and eases your mental burden.

On the alternative factor, letting flow into takes bravery and could. It involves letting cross of your attachment in your anxieties and giving them time to pass. This give up is a announcement of energy as opposed to weak spot. I'll stroll you thru every step of the exercise and give you the competencies you need to permit skip of your fears and deliver your mind a breather.

Resources for Fostering Inner Peace

You may have a toolkit whole of techniques for developing inner calm as you located out for your course to inner peace. These resources mild your way via even the darkest intellectual storms, similar to beacons. They will allow you to take command of your mind and emotions all all over again.

You'll come to rely upon respiratory wearing sports, rest techniques and meditation sports activities. These tools have been subtle and polished over decades, imparting infinite human beings with comfort and peace of thoughts. I will not handiest disclose you to those procedures as a consultant in this area, but I may provide you useful advice on the way to comprise them into your normal regular.

The course to internal serenity is a in no manner-completing adventure in preference to a very last holiday spot. It calls for commitment, repetition and an openness to trade. But the praise is well truely honestly really worth the attempt: a lifestyles of peace, clarity and a revitalized revel in of direction. Come along with me as we discover the ones lifestyles-changing techniques in the imminent chapters, uncovering the energy of popularity, mindfulness and the strategies for developing internal peace. We will move with a bit of success and purposefully together down the direction that consequences in inner serenity that awaits you.

Practical Techniques for Quieting the Mind

Developing a toolset of useful techniques to forestall the thoughts's ordinary chatter is vital to overcome overthinking. To begin this street of transformation, you want to first learn how to get better manage over your thoughts and quiet the chatter that keeps you mired in uncertainty and fear.

Deep breathing carrying sports, grounding strategies and mindfulness practices are useful strategies for calming the mind. When used constantly, these belongings allow you to in regaining attention and letting skip of your tendency to overthink. I'll walk you through every exercising, offering recommendation and steerage along the way that will help you benefit the highbrow fortitude needed to manipulate your mind.

Being steady is vital. As a expert on this area, I've witnessed innumerable human beings change their lives via adopting the ones practices into their ordinary schedules. By doing this, you could lay the idea for intellectual peace, on the way to can help you confront overthinking head-on.

Dismantling Adverse Thought Patterns

Negative idea behavior that have been imprinted profoundly over the years are regularly the motive of overthinking. These notion patterns increase anxiety, feed self-doubt and make it hard to take into account your judgment. Identifying those inclinations and taking them on head-on is the second one approach for overcoming overthinking.

We will artwork together to discover the manner to understand those unstable idea patterns, which consist of self-complaint, black-and-white wondering and catastrophizing. You'll discover how to investigate and query these belief styles with a view to change them out for delivered realistic and useful ones. Through this approach, you will be capable of take returned manage of your thoughts and reduce the affect that overthinking has in your life.

One of the maximum essential matters you can do to go inside the path of internal peace is to discover ways to confront poor thinking behavior. You will note a large exchange in the manner you view and have interaction with the area as you face and conquer those conduct.

Developing Love for Oneself

A key to overcoming overthinking is to practice self-compassion. Many those who war with overthinking also are their very non-public worst critics, punishing themselves for perceived shortcomings and retaining themselves to now not feasible requirements. The overthinking loop is fueled thru this self-essential perspective.

Treating your self with the equal interest and facts which you might likely make bigger to an remarkable friend is the muse of cultivating self-compassion. It entails knowing that everyone makes mistakes and reviews intervals of uncertainty and that perfection is an phantasm. You can build a safety in opposition to overthinking's self-detrimental inclinations thru training self-compassion.

I'll lead you thru sports activities and introspection to assist the increase of self-compassion. You'll find out the way to quiet your inner critic and begin talking to your self in a kinder, extra loving way. This change will decorate your emotional fitness and mind-set on existence further to relieving you of the want to overthink everything.

Your door to regaining mental freedom and enduring internal calm is thru mastering overthinking strategies. You can unfastened up yourself from the shackles of overthinking and experience a life of readability and tranquility via way of reading useful techniques for stilling the mind, confronting bad idea styles and developing self-compassion. Come alongside aspect me as we study those undertaking-converting strategies and set off on a direction to a happier, more non violent future.

## MASTERING THE ART OF WORRY MANAGEMENT

Stress Reduction and Relaxation Techniques

Learning to lessen tension and loosen up is step one inside the route of growing fear control skills, which is probably vital to getting to know the paintings of letting skip. Our lives are overflowing with duties, closing dates and goals, that might provide an wonderful surroundings for worry to proliferate. We should discover ways to calm the stress storm in advance than we are able to calm the priority storm.

Your wonderful defence in opposition to the everyday stresses of contemporary life is to workout rest and pressure reduction. By turning into proficient in the ones techniques, you'll be able to stop tension from taking preserve in addition to lowering the emotional and physical effects of stress. I will stroll you through the manner of making relaxation strategies, which incorporates present day muscle rest, deep breathing sporting activities and mindfulness-based absolutely pressure bargain, as I am an expert on this concern.

When you observe the ones strategies on your ordinary lifestyles, you'll be capable of rebuild resilience and equilibrium. You'll end up more adept at navigating lifestyles's storms and coping with your fear becomes a vital aspect of your quest for internal peace.

Establishing a Stress-Free Space

An critical however from time to time left out a part of handling tension is putting in place a fear-free environment. Our surroundings substantially influences how we sense, therefore a good manner to turn out to be adept at letting pass, we want to create a vicinity that encourages us on our direction to internal serenity.

We'll have a have a study strategies for putting limits, organizing your artwork and clearing out your bodily place. You may additionally additionally moreover create a relaxed and serene region by way of simplifying your environment and decreasing outside elements that might purpose you to overthink and worry.

It is viable to create an environment loose from worry outdoor of the physical worldwide. It consists of growing a community of pals and own family who're there to useful resource you, preserving suitable relationships and talking successfully. These components are crucial to your ability to govern anxiety and hold highbrow clarity.

The Significance of Adaptability and Resilience

Resilience and adaptability are essential components of inner energy whilst gaining knowledge of problem manage. Difficulties are a given in existence for the reason that existence is erratic. While model allows you thrive in the face of exchange, resilience permits you get over setbacks.

I'll educate you techniques for strengthening your emotional fortitude and improving your hassle-fixing talents, in addition to techniques for developing resilience and flexibility. You'll discover a way to look failures as possibilities for private improvement in region of as reasons for concern.

Resilience and version have an effect on society as a whole, collectively together with your relationships and career. Their significance goes past the man or woman. You can assemble a life that is greater bendy, more capable of navigating the unknowns of the destiny and lots less prone to fear with the useful resource of developing these trends.

We will move into amazing detail on the nuances of worry control on this segment, presenting you with the competencies and information you want to quiet the clamor of fear and open the door to internal serenity. You will make massive improvement inside the direction of a lifestyles characterized through mental clarity and emotional resilience through embracing strain cut charge and relaxation practices, putting in a worry-unfastened surroundings and strengthening your resilience and versatility. Come along facet me in this enlightening journey as we together study the art of project manipulate.

## Chapter 10: Cultivating Mental Clarity

Concentration and Focus's Power

Developing highbrow readability is the lighthouse that points the manner to a purposeful and non violent lifestyles. Developing the functionality to consciousness and listen is essential in modern-day rapid-paced environment, even as there are numerous distractions and the mind regularly seems like a stormy sea.

Our potential to simplify our mind and consciousness our intellectual strength on the right right here and now is facilitated by manner of awareness and awareness. When evolved, the ones talents act as a counterbalance to the mayhem that results from overanalyzing, allowing us to break out the bonds of chronic ruminating.

I will percent my records as a consultant on this region to help you enhance your interest and attention. You'll find out beneficial techniques and sports activities activities that assist you take back control of your having a pipe dream mind. You will benefit the talents critical to become an expert at attention thru mindfulness bodily video video games and targeted training, allowing you to create a sanctuary of intellectual clarity on your everyday life.

Techniques for Making Decisions

The worst effect overthinking has on our ability to make picks is surely simply one among the biggest problems it gives. The in no way-finishing loop of uncertainty and self-evaluation impairs our functionality to make choices with assurance and clarity. Developing suitable selection-making techniques is inextricably linked to cultivating intellectual readability.

We shall have a look at the fundamentals of nicely-knowledgeable choice-making on this component. You'll find out a way to compare alternatives, set up priorities and carefully consider the blessings and drawbacks of each alternative. Improved strategies for making choices will help you are making picks quicker and with masses a lot much less emotional upheaval from doubt and ambiguity.

By turning into gifted inside the ones techniques, you will create the premise for a life free from the weight of immoderate evaluation and characterised with the useful useful resource of readability and decisiveness.

Improved Capabilities for Solving Problems

The ability to remedy problems efficiently is the sign of highbrow clarity. It is a skill that gives us the capability to with a bit of luck and poised negotiate the complexities of existence and meet obstacles head-on. Our potential to clear up problems efficiently is regularly hampered by means of the use of overthinking, as it can snare us in a maze of useless tension and self-doubt.

I will offer you an in depth toolkit to enhance your trouble-fixing abilities because of the reality I am an professional within the company. We will explore techniques for dissecting elaborate troubles, comparing viable fixes and formulating a methodical method for trouble-solving. These skills will help you expand a sturdy enjoy of empowerment and self-assure similarly to growing you a extra skilled problem solver.

Developing highbrow clarity consists of planned attempt to decorate your capability to recognition, make alternatives more fast and clear up problems greater effectively. It isn't a passive method. Gaining mastery over the ones elements of highbrow readability will open the door to a beneficial and decisive lifestyles. Come at the side of me as we study the transformational potential of interest, judgment and hassle-solving strategies and together allow's circulate on a path inside the path of a existence characterised through manner of way of resilience and highbrow readability.

OVERCOMING OBSTACLES AND RELAPSES

Dealing with Relapses and Setbacks

Learning to permit circulates of strain and overthinking is a manner that is not constantly sincere. That's a non-forestall device and setbacks and relapses are possible. The mystery to real mastery, even though, is to apprehend a way to cope with the ones situations in location of trying to avoid them.

The capability to address screw ups and relapses is important in case you need to achieve long-lasting inner calm. You'll broaden the capability to become aware of at the same time as you are reverting to antique sporting events and use realistic strategies to get decrease returned heading within the proper course. I will provide you the abilties to recognize the early caution signs and symptoms of a relapse and reroute your path again within the direction of clarity and calmness as a subject rely variety expert in this area.

Being able to cope with disasters and relapses is a sign of energy in region of weak point. It is an essential a part of your adventure, education you to truly receive flaws and press on with persistence.

Handling Stressors from Without

Stressors from with out are an unavoidable problem of life. They can also originate from pretty some resources, together with relationships, employment and health. It is crucial that you manage the ones stressors if you need to maintain your newly advanced resilience and highbrow clarity.

We should have a look at useful strategies in this trouble for dealing with pressure from outdoor resources. You'll find out a way to address existence's limitations via getting to know the way to set limits, make reasonable expectancies and use stress-discount techniques. By becoming talented in the ones strategies, you could assemble the resilience required to resist out of doors impacts without giving in to anxiety and overanalyzing.

Recall that the cause is to decorate your functionality to manipulate pressures on your lifestyles with out sacrificing your internal peace. It isn't about disposing of them.

Creating a Network of Support

Nobody want to journey by myself looking for internal tranquility. Creating a community of help is the closing crucial to your fulfillment. A beneficial aid device, whether or not it comes from buddies, own family, or a collection of folks that percent your values, is essential to overcoming setbacks and relapses.

I will help you in growing a robust resource community due to the fact I am an professional on this vicinity. We'll talk about a manner to particular your desires, ask for help whilst you need it and construct a useful resource system of folks who get you on this direction.

When topics pass tough, your network of help will characteristic a safety net, presenting you motivation, mind-set and reassurance which you're no longer the fine one pursuing resilience and mental readability.

We will talk the significance of managing setbacks and relapses, overcoming outside stressors and growing a manual network in this final section. These are the abilties that will help you keep your newly observed internal serenity on the same time as navigating the issues which might be positive to upward push up. Come discover with me the transformational power of network, coping strategies and resilience. Together, we're going to take the closing steps towards living a existence characterized through enduring intellectual clarity and emotional properly-being.

LIVING A LIFE OF FULFILLMENT AND FREEDOM

Setting and Achieving Personal Goals

The motive of reading the method of letting move of strain and overthinking is to live a existence of success and freedom. It's a existence characterised thru accomplishment, because of this and deep pleasure. Setting and attractive in private goals is step one at the direction to this vacation spot.

Individual desires are the benchmarks that strain us in advance and provide us a sense of motive. Our lives are unique and our movements are stimulated through our hopes, aspirations and desires. You will discover a manner to create workable, beneficial dreams that complement your ideals and pursuits in this element.

I will help you in growing a clean avenue map to your destiny by means of manner of the usage of guiding you thru the goal-putting technique as a topic depend expert in this vicinity. We'll have a examine strategies for dividing extra bold dreams into practicable chunks and retaining motivation as we pass.

You might be free of the restrictions of overanalyzing and worrying if you may broaden a purposeful and directed life and examine the paintings of making and sporting out private dreams.

Fostering an Understanding of Meaning and Purpose

A actual enjoy of which means that that and cause is critical for a existence of achievement and freedom. It is the beacon of mild that brightens your manner and gives each day which means. Finding and growing this experience of purpose is a essential step in your direction to a extra fulfilling life.

You will discover a way to discover your internal values, beliefs and passions on this segment. You will exit on a voyage of self-discovery to find the special competencies and contributions you may provide to the area. You will find out the way to deliver your life that means and cause, out of your relationships to your art work, beneath the route of a expert.

Living a lifestyles that is triggered with the useful resource of your innermost beliefs and desires requires growing a enjoy of which means and reason. You might be absolutely thrilled at the side of your lifestyles and locate achievement in all which you do if you instill this experience of motive into each day.

Adopting a Happy and Stress-Free Life

Finally, you may gather the very satisfactory aspect on your route: residing a happy, fear-unfastened existence. This is your task fulfilled, the surrender quit result of all of the paintings you placed into learning a way to allow bypass.

You will very own the abilities to liberate yourself from the regulations of anxiety and overanalyzing with the aid of the use of placing the requirements and strategies referred to on this e-book into exercise. You might also have advanced the abilities to deal with lifestyles's boundaries gracefully and with resiliency. Additionally, you'll have determined out a way to apply highbrow readability to treatment issues, make alternatives and joyfully get delight from each second.

You can consist of a satisfied, fear-loose existence thru developing a determination to non-public improvement, evolution and self-focus. It is a lifestyles that exudes positivity, this means that and freedom from the shackles of unnecessary fear.

This final segment will talk the pleasures of residing existence to the fullest, which incorporates achieving private dreams, having a deep feel of which means that and purpose and experiencing the sheer, unadulterated pleasure of dwelling worry-loose. Come have an exquisite time with me the adventure's transformative strength and allow's take the last steps in the direction of a existence full of freedom and lengthy-lasting fulfillment.